Historic
JACKSONVILLE
THEATRE PALACES, DRIVE-INS AND MOVIE HOUSES

DOROTHY K. FLETCHER

THE History PRESS

Published by The History Press
Charleston, SC
www.historypress.net

First published 2015

Manufactured in the United States

ISBN 978.1.62619.770.1

Library of Congress Control Number: 2015950739

In memory of Byron W. Riggan.

CONTENTS

INTRODUCTION

All the world's a stage,
And all the men and women merely players.
—William Shakespeare, As You Like It, *act 2, scene 7*

There were many reasons why I was drawn to writing a book about Jacksonville theatres. To begin with, my father had a passion for movies. Whether we were in a theatre, a car at the drive-in or just sitting on the sofa at home watching the Sunday movie matinee on television, his love for movies was infectious. His childhood favorites—*Tarzan*, *Captain Blood*, *Beau Geste*—became my favorites, and I came to appreciate all the war movies he took us to watch like *The Guns of Navarone*, *The Young Lions* and *The Caine Mutiny*.

My mother was into live productions and musical performances, and she helped me come to appreciate plays and concerts. On many an afternoon, we enjoyed *Peter and the Wolf*, the *Nutcracker Suite* or *A Midsummer Night's Dream*. She opened the world of music and dance and drama to me.

As a teenager, I discovered I had independence, and my best friend, Marguerite, and I hopped a bus to get to the Center Theatre at least four times to be swept away by the epic movie *Lawrence of Arabia*. Oh, how my father would tease me about my fanatic devotion for Peter O'Toole! Still, he didn't discourage my going since he knew very well the lure of motion pictures, especially grand ones.

I discovered the fun of drive-ins when I was a little bit older—meeting friends, boyfriends, hiding in the trunk. What more can I say?

When I became a parent, the cycle began again. My children learned to love movies and the wonderful places that showed them. We went to plays and concerts and drive-ins and movie houses, and my daughter even became a concessionaire at the long-gone Baymeadows Eight Movie Theatre. Every night, she came home smelling of popcorn, and that smell instantly took me back to earlier days when we all "went out to the lobby, to get ourselves a treat."

It was only natural that I would gravitate toward this project.

When I started, I knew that I would have to sort through a great deal of information, but I wasn't expecting the scope of that information to become so massive. After a while, I began to experience something akin to what I have imagined herding cattle might be like. The bulk of the information just loped along at a steady pace when all of a sudden I'd realize that three cows (or topics) had wandered off in different contrary directions. It took hours for me to get back to the herd (or the manuscript). Then, there'd be a stampede that would take me totally by surprise and would upset all my original plans so that I had to start over.

There were the lonely moments when I wondered how I got into this "cattle drive" in the first place and the ecstatic moments when I discovered wonderful places and things I would never have experienced had I not signed up for the trip. It has been quite the "drive" for me.

As with all books, I needed to find a method of organization, and four major sections slowly emerged, although they do tend to overlap. Chapter 1 deals with theatres around the first quarter of the twentieth century: the vaudeville, nickelodeons, early moving pictures and formal theatrical and concert venues. I felt it necessary to honor the very old theatres that have been dust longer than most of us have been alive. These theatres set the groundwork for all the theatres that followed. Chapter 2 covers live performance theatres, many of which are still operating and entertaining us today. Chapter 3 covers many of the movie theatres that thrived in the mid- to late twentieth century, and finally, Chapter 4 pays homage to the drive-in movie phenomenon.

Please be advised that I will not be including multiplex theatres, nor have I covered every theatre that ever existed in Jacksonville. Sadly, I have left out a number of theatres for which I could find very little information. Sometimes theatres began with one name and closed with another, and some were forbidden places that banned young people for obvious reasons. I took what information I could find, and hopefully, the most memorable theatres are represented.

There is a piece of housekeeping I need to address—the spelling of the word *theatre*. Throughout this book, I will use the British spelling of the word; first, because Robert Arleigh White, retired executive director for Theatre Jacksonville, former Cultural Council director and present-day actor, told me so. "Theatre" is how the word should always be spelled!

There is also another reason. The theatres represented in this book used the British spelling in advertizing and on their marquees. The print media used that spelling in almost every article or review I researched. Therefore, I will use the British spelling in this book since it wasn't until more recent times that the American spelling of the word crept into usage and into being the preferred spelling in the dictionary.

With all of that being said, I hope I have covered all your favorite theatres and that my chapters will conjure many happy memories. All that's left to do now is to sit back in a nice comfy chair and enjoy once again the magic of Jacksonville's most memorable theatres.

1

EARLY JACKSONVILLE THEATRES

LONG-GONE THEATRES

One can only imagine what it was like in Jacksonville in 1900. It was certain to have had a far different landscape and feel about it. Horses were still used in the transport of goods and people, trolleys rumbled down tracks and automobiles were few and far between. Air conditioning was still in the future, but the electric fan had thankfully been invented. And the citizens of Jacksonville had a different sophistication level when it came to entertainment. Minstrel shows, vaudevillian acts, recitations and magic acts were all the rage back in those earlier times.

As I began my research of Jacksonville theatres, I found two outstanding articles, both written by Dick Bussard, city editor of the *Jacksonville Journal*. The first article is called "When the Nickelodeon Was in Flower," which ran on May 15, 1975. Bussard not only provided one of the best chronologies of the film industry but also interviewed two Jacksonville projectionists from the earliest years of motion pictures in our city.

According to Bussard, Thomas Edison invented the kinetoscope in 1894. In 1895, the first motion picture was shown to an audience in Paris. In 1903, *The Great Train Robbery*—the first full-length motion picture—premiered, and in 1907, nickelodeons were the only "movies" in Jacksonville. The article noted: "Most Nickelodeons were small storefronts and according to Cawthon [one of the projectionists interviewed], consisted of a projector, a screen and a few chairs. Some provided a piano accompanist and all charged a nickel, thus the name. They also were noted for their gaudy advertising posters outside."

The article went on to say that regular theatres of the first quarter of the century were usually vaudeville houses with proscenium arch stages. As motion pictures developed, these theatres would use "movies" to fill in between acts. One such theatre was the Phoenix Park Theatre at 411 West Bay Street. Miss Mabel Paige and her big stock company opened here, and the films used between performances were *Master and Man* and *The Shadow*.

By 1910, according to the article, Jacksonville theatres really began to blossom. There was the Orpheum Theatre (which, when it closed, became the building housing the Young Men's Shop). There was also the Majestic Theatre at 201 West Bay, the Pastime Theatre at 215 West Bay Street and the Lyric Theatre at 113 Main Street. The Amusu Theatre on Forsyth Street near Main was a big vaudeville venue that would eventually become the Grand Theatre. The Duval Theatre would eventually become the Temple Theatre.

Bussard pointed out that on the day the *Lusitania* sank, May 7, 1915, motion pictures and vaudeville were flourishing in Jacksonville even though many of the nickelodeons had passed on. Theda Bara was starring at the Republic Theatre in *The Vampire*, and the Cycling Brunettes were performing "a series of difficult tricks" at the Orpheum Theatre. The Grand Theatre was showing *Dopey Chaplin*, starring, of all people, Charlie Chaplin.

By the time we were in the middle of World War II, things had evolved. The article said, "The Temple was still a vaudeville theatre, but it no longer was Jacksonville's coolest and best. Often there were more performers on stage than there were customers in the audience. And you knew that vaudeville wasn't dying, it was already dead."

According to the article, there was only one theatre from those early days in Jacksonville that was still operating as a theatre—the Arcade Theatre, opened in 1914. This venue would become the Center Theatre in the '60s.

Bussard's article also contained interviews with two projectionists: Elvin Pratt and Bender A. (Dock) Cawthon. Pratt was sixteen when he became a projectionist at the 20th Century Theatre on Bridge Street (now called Broad Street), and he retired after fifty-seven years at a variety of theatres—the last one being the Edgewood Theatre. At the time of the article's publication, Dock Cawthon was still working at the Florida Theatre in its seventy-seat screening room. He had begun his career in 1922.

One interesting tidbit about the job of early projectionists was revealed in the *Journal* article: "Cawthon said that in the early days movie film was fed through the projector and spilled into a basket after which it was rolled back onto the reel. But because of the highly flammable nature of film—fires

Longtime projectionist at the Center Theatre Jake Rekoth. *Courtesy of Ellen Ruffner Pierce.*

were common in those days—the reels were eventually enclosed in metal boxes as a safety measure."

As often happens when I do research, I got excited about finding a picture to go with my text. Ellen Ruffner Pierce, whose father had been manager at a number of downtown theatres, provided me with a great image of a projectionist who had worked with her father, and I couldn't wait to use it. I thought it was a picture of Dock Cawthon; however, I was wrong, and I am so glad I double checked. I contacted the Florida Theatre, and Bob Christopher, who had been a projectionist at the Florida Theatre for many years, identified the image as that of Jake Rekoth. Rekoth had been the secretary-treasurer of the IATSE Projectionist Union, Local 511. In any case, the picture shows what the world of a projectionist was like.

Dick Bussard's second article was entitled "City's 'Theatre Row' Is No More." It ran on September 27, 1971, and in it, he extolled the wonder of Jacksonville's little piece of theatre magic and bemoaned the loss of two theatre icons: the Empress and the Imperial Theatres. He said, "Forsyth Street was truly 'theatre row.' At night the theatre lights lit up the sky like a little Broadway, at least for a few blocks."

He went on to say, "There was a time not long ago when you passed five other theatres if you walked from the Center to the Florida. And there were several more within a block or two in other directions."

He explained that the Empress was built right after the 1901 fire and the Imperial came along in 1907. The Rialto was at Main and Forsyth Streets. On the other side of the Imperial was the Palace, a place where Bussard once stood in line to see Eddie Arnold in person. Then, there was the Center (which had once been the Arcade), and across the street was the Roxy. There was a comparatively new theatre also on Forsyth called the St. Johns, which showed *The Pride of the Yankees* as one of its first films.

A block away on Bay Street stood the Casino, which eventually became "a male-only type theatre that showed burlesque movies." A short distance from Forsyth on Main Street was the Temple Theatre, where "vaudeville had its last gasp in Jacksonville," and north from there on Main Street was the Capitol Theatre.

When this article was written, only the Florida and the Center Theatres remained of Jacksonville's theatre row. The once thriving theatre district had only these two left.

Even after reading both of these articles, I could see that gaps existed in the information. Not every theatre that operated in Jacksonville was mentioned in these articles. One very important theatre was left out.

Savoy Theatre, early 1900s. *Courtesy of the Florida State Photographic Archives.*

In an article that began with "Do you remember when you went to the movies in this theatre?" published in the *Jacksonville Journal* on December 31, 1937, the reporter mentioned an early moving picture house called the Savoy Theatre at the corner of Main and Forsyth Streets. According to the article, the Savoy and an unnamed theatre across the street were the only two motion picture houses in the city in 1910.

The article said that John T. Alsop, for whom our Main Street Bridge is named and who was a city councilman who would eventually become mayor, converted a two-storied building into a theatre named the Savoy Theatre.

Alsop, Robert J. Chambers and Pete Kontos leased the property from owner Harold Weston for ninety-nine years. Eventually, the Lynch Building would replace the theatre in 1927. When the theatre was built, it had a seating capacity of four hundred. In those days, a program consisted of three reels, each lasting about ten minutes. Alsop owned and operated the Savoy for about ten years, and W.L. Whitehead was the manager.

So many of the theatres in the early part of the twentieth century winked in and out of existence without much fanfare, but just reading their names—the Star, the Mirror, the Princess, the Prince, the Hippodrome, the Bijou and the Colonial Theatres—made me envision a rich landscape of entertainment for those who lived in Jacksonville ever so long ago.

ARCADE THEATRE/CENTER THEATRE

The Arcade Theatre at 41 West Forsyth Street and 30½ West Adams Street was, according to an article in the *Jacksonville Journal* written by Dick Bussard and published on September 27, 1971, opened in 1914 and was "originally a vaudeville and legitimate theatre." It also said the theatre got its name "because there was an arcade running through the middle of the block between Adams and Forsyth. There were ticket windows on both blocks."

Bussard's article noted that a "boy could take his first date on a bus to the Arcade and see a Gene Autrey movie and still have enough money for two boxes of popcorn."

When the Empress and the Imperial Theatres were demolished in Jacksonville in 1971 and the *Jacksonville Journal* ran Bussard's story about it, they were surprised that it "resulted in an unusual response from residents who offered additional information" in the form of letters.

One such letter came from Circuit Court judge Frank H. Elmore, and it was so informative that the *Journal* published his long letter as an article with a byline on November 4, 1971. He mentioned, among others, the Arcade Theatre, saying that it was for a number of years "the home of a local stock company which presented popular plays. Among its stars were Guy Combs, who had been a star with the Kalem Company in the days of moving picture production in Jacksonville (1907–15) and Ed Lawrence, a local man noted for his silver hair."

In a more modern time, one spectacular event occurred at the Arcade Theatre. Dr. Wally Eaton, a professor of Cyber Forensics at Florida State College–Jacksonville, told me about it. He said, "When *The Pride and the Passion* was being shown at this theatre, my sister was an usherette on the staff. This high-budget movie was advertised as being in both Technicolor and Vistavision. Its stars included Cary Grant, Frank Sinatra and Sophia Loren. During the film's run, the manager, a go-getter of a promoter, publicized the movie by blocking off half of the street and having shipped from Hollywood the actual gigantic cannon that was the main prop of the film."

Some two years later, the Arcade Theatre would close and then reopen as the Center Theatre. An article announcing the grand reopening was carried in the *Florida Times-Union* on August 3, 1960. According to the piece, written by Judge May, the Arcade closed on June 6, 1960, and the renovation project began so that the new theatre would be "completely redesigned and renovated." When it reopened on Wednesday, August 3, 1960, it was one of the "most modern motion picture houses in the Southeast with a new wide screen, new seats, a new sound system, and redesigned lobby and auditorium."

Then, on August 7, 1960, Judge May published a review of the grand reopening. He said that the movie *Ben-Hur*—a $15 million production that had already garnered eleven Academy Award nominations, including Best Picture—was a logical choice for an opening film since it would match the "splendor of the new Center Theatre." That renovation cost $100,000.

He went on to say, "In its new dress, it is one of the most modern theatres in the state. New seats have been installed throughout, a modern foyer and lobby have been installed and it now contains the most modern sound and projection equipment available."

Just imagine that you are sitting in the darkened auditorium of a theatre on opening night. Then, in the hush that follows, the curtains are drawn back and an ancient reality comes into focus. *Ben-Hur* was shot with new 65mm widescreen technology, and it didn't take long for audiences to be enveloped in the dazzling sights and majestic sounds of Roman legions, breathtaking chariot races, sea battles between great ships and miraculous events—all this and Charlton Heston, too.

Such was the experience of many citizens of Jacksonville at the newly renovated Center Theatre. It was such a momentous occasion that the patrons were provided with bound programs that were filled with stories of how the film was made and stills of the cast and crew.

For twenty-three years, the Center Theatre continued to be profitable, until the mid-'60s. In an article that ran in the *Jacksonville Journal* on January 6, 1983, Beau Halton announced that the Center Theatre had closed its doors.

Halton spoke with Bob Jones, district manager for Plitt Southern Theatres in Orlando, who said, "Sure it was the last theatre in downtown Jacksonville...But like everyone else, we had to look at the economic realities." Later in the article, he said, "Single-screened theatres are like dinosaurs nowadays...They are just completely outdated. People haven't been coming the way they used to."

Then, in an article written by Tia Mitchell in the *Florida Times-Union* on September 6, 2002, we are told: "The 90-year-old building [that had once housed the Center Theatre] partially collapsed sometime during the early morning hours. Though transients were believed to occasionally inhabit the abandoned building and surrounding areas, no one was hurt."

All those wonderful movie hours spent in the grandeur of spectacular dramas went up in a cloud of dust that night. As with all things, it certainly epitomized the harsh march of time, even on those things we cherish in memory.

CAPITOL THEATRE

I encountered the Capitol Theatre in a few articles, but it was mostly mentioned in passing. So I was delighted when I heard from Margaret Rose, whose father, William, is a Southside resident who retired from the food industry. She told me in an e-mail a special story about his experiences at the Capitol when he was a little boy:

> *He* [her father, William Rose] *grew up in Springfield, several blocks from the Capitol Theatre, which was located on Main Street, between Seventh and Eighth Streets. His father would give him a dime for the movie and a penny for the gumball machine. One Saturday, when he was eight or nine—so that would have been 1934 or 1935—he went to the theatre*

> *to see what he thinks was* Little Orphan Annie. *There was a long line going all the way around the block. While waiting in line, he held on tightly to the coin his dad had given him. He finally got to the front of the line, and placed the coin on the counter. The cashier said "Son, the movie is a dime, and this is a penny." It was then that he realized that he must have put the dime in the gumball machine by mistake. He never did see the movie.*

Another great piece of information I found about the Capitol Theatre came from a woman named Shirley Jordan Gardner. She is not a Hollywood icon, nor is her name on the lips of many people around here anymore. She died on April 23, 2011, at the age of eighty, and her brief obituary ran in the *Florida Times-Union*. All it said was that she was born on October 7, 1930; she had attended Andrew Jackson High School; and she went to the University of Florida. She had worked for the Florida Bureau of Water and Swimming Pool Department, and she was survived by two sons—Roy W. Gardner and Keith H. Gardner.

I mention her here because of a letter she wrote to the editor of the *Metropolis.* I discovered a Xeroxed copy of it in an obscure folder in a vertical file of the Jacksonville Downtown Public Library, and as I read it, I was immediately touched.

Hers was not a political letter, nor was it a complaint. Instead, it was almost a love letter written on the occasion of the "death" of one of Jacksonville's core city theatres—the Capitol.

This letter, published on February, 9, 1983, extolled the virtues of being a kid in Jacksonville and getting to enjoy, with throngs of other children, the wonders of the Capitol Theatre. She said:

> *When I wasn't looking, someone went in with a wrecker's ball and demolished my theatre, my center for the performing arts: the Capitol movie theatre.*
>
> *As a kid I didn't know a whole bunch about the performing arts, except the Capitol. Many actors performed and they were artists.*
>
> *The land where my theatre stood at 1941 Main Street between Seventh and Eighth is a mini-rubble strewn canyon. The Capitol was there for me only a block from where I grew up.*

She would go on to tell us how nice it was having a theatre so close to home. She could be there on afternoons and evenings and most certainly for the Saturday matinees. She could even leave through an exit into an alley where she could buy ice cream and soft drinks.

Capitol Theatre, 1927. *Courtesy of the Florida State Photographic Archives.*

When she was a teenager in the 1940s, she worked at the Capitol selling popcorn and tickets, and she was able to see many movies as a result. She described how teens flocked there since gasoline and cars were hard to come by in those days. They walked and biked and rode the bus to meet their friends at the Capitol. She, and many others, had a few first dates there.

She also mentions how she and her friends giggled a lot about the "mild romances" playing out in the back rows, with the ushers always ready to hush and remove wrongdoers.

> *At the time, I never thought my world of Celluloid, escape and fantasy could end. I was sure I would grow up, somehow sing like Judy Garland, dance like Ginger Rogers and act like Bette Davis. I could very easily consider the possibility of marrying Charles Boyer, or solve the world's problems by being a brilliant scientist, inventor or missionary. Even with the reality of working and the outside world* way, way *in the back of my mind, the actors, their characters and lives were secretly attainable to my romantic, sentimental, adolescent heart.*

But her final paragraphs encapsulated the very essence of what going to the movies was all about, and her lament really resonated with me.

> *In my mind's eye, I see that single empty lot on the block where my theatre stood, in which I spent so many hours. But I also see people lined down the sidewalk, all ages (we didn't need to be concerned about ratings then) waiting for the next show to begin. I smell popcorn smothered in butter and feel the anticipation of seeing a new movie, cheering the good guys, booing the bad; laughing, crying, dreaming…*

Shirley Jordan Gardner might not have been a household name, but she certainly captured in her letter what wonders theatres could bring to appreciative audiences. And I couldn't let her views be lost to time, as they articulate so well what we all felt about our neighborhood theatres.

CASINO THEATRE

Whenever I ask anyone of an age about the Casino Theatre, I get the impression that it had a rather "seedy" reputation. Not only did it end up a "girly" theatre, according to Dick Bussard's *Journal* article written in 1975, but it also had other stories that made me wonder.

I spoke on the telephone on December 30, 2014, with Buddy Ross, retired finance and budget control supervisor of public works for the city of Jacksonville. He had so many wonderful movie memories, most of which revolved around his group of six friends. They would skate everywhere—from Post Street over the Lee Street Viaduct to Bay Street, where the Casino Theatre was. It cost each of them five cents to get in.

Ross said:

> *My father was a policeman, a traffic cop who directed traffic at Main and Bay or Main and Forsyth or Main and Adams. He didn't want me going to the Casino Theatre, but we went there anyway, and he never found us out; at least he never said anything to us. I guess he didn't want us there because it was not the cleanest place in the world. There was a lot of devilment going on there since it was mostly kids and teenagers. Cokes had spilt on the floors, and there was lots of gum under the seats. Nothing ever got cleaned, and they never mopped the floor. And there were rats the size of the horses in the westerns that we loved to watch.*

Still, Ross and his buddies went back time and again. He said, "We couldn't wait to see how the serials would turn out—cliffhangers like *The Lone Ranger* and *Flash Gordon*; and then there would be the features. We mostly loved the westerns."

There are other accounts of what went on there. Dr. Wally Eaton, professor at FSCJ, told me that he still has his grandparents' green Depression glass cookie jar that they won as a door prize at the Casino Theatre during the 1930s. Since each person has a different set of perceptions about any given person, place or thing, memories of theatres are certain to vary widely as well.

DIXIE THEATRE

The Dixie Theatre was located at Mary Street just off the Main Street Bridge on the Southbank of the St. Johns River. It was originally part of the Dixieland Park complex, which had been built in 1907. Deborah Webb Rogers is a teacher at Douglas Anderson and is a history writer who is presently doing research for a third book on Dixieland Park.

According to her, "Dixieland Park was billed as the 'Coney Island of the South.' It was part of the boom of trolley parks which had destinations at the end of the line. It also had many of the same things that the New York Coney Island had—a Dreamland and there was even a scientific exhibition of babies in incubators."

An article written by Bill Foley and published on September 3, 1964, in the *Florida Times-Union* announced the demolition of the old building with the headline "Razing of Old Dixie Theatre Begins." The article said:

> *It was 1907 when the Dixie Theatre opened. It was in the heart of the Dixieland Park, a playground "better than a carnival because it was always there."*
>
> *The theatre was the focal point of the park, drawing as much attention as the Japanese acrobats, the roller coaster and the 160-foot bamboo slide.*
>
> *It* [the theatre] *housed Dixieland band concerts, more refined concerts, operas, plays, lectures, sermons and social event after social event. Duval High School ferried its graduates across the river for commencement exercises.*

Sadly, the appeal of Dixieland Park and its theatre began to fade by 1909, and when there were fewer and fewer acts coming there, the neighborhood began to encroach on the property. "The lights went out on the Treaty Oak and they stopped shooting fireworks in Dixieland Park."

Rogers said that interest in the park probably faded out since one had to cross the river by ferry to get there, and that was a bit of an undertaking for most Jacksonville citizens in those days.

There were those who talked of turning the theatre into a movie studio, and that worked for a while, but eventually the theatre building was used for

Old Dixie Theatre in Dixieland Park, early 1900s. *Courtesy of the Jacksonville Historical Society.*

dances and basketball games. The Boston Celtics played there in the '30s. Its most recent use was as a skating rink. Then, in 1964, the theatre was torn down by the P.L. Burkhalter Company, for no particular reason. The article said, "It's coming down because people are tired of it being there and would rather have a little space."

PALACE THEATRE

Just as many of the older theatres were, the Palace Theatre was a full theatrical venue, and its primary form of entertainment when it opened was vaudeville shows. On January 15, 1967, an article that was written by Sharon Gould ran in the *Times/Journal* Magazine of the *Florida Times Union.* She talked at length about the Palace and the kind of entertainment that it promoted.

Along with relaying interviews with vaudevillian actors, Gould said that the Palace was built in 1918 by S.A. Lynch, president of Lynch Enterprises. It was, as the article says, on the famous Keith Albee circuit, booking more big-time performers than local theatres.

Gould gave a very interesting rundown of how an evening of vaudeville performances might go:

> *A song and dance team kicked the show into high gear, maybe with a snappy buck and swing, a sentimental balladeer crooned "When the Blue Birds Nest Again, Sweet Nellie Gray," "Dear Old Girl," or maybe a rousing "Are you from Dixie?" A comedy sketch preceded a monologist followed by a character specialty (like rope-twirling, wise-cracking Will Rogers or juggler-joke-teller W.C. Fields who both played Jacksonville); then a short dramatic skit led up to a headliner (Eva Tanguay, the "I Don't Care Girl" and comedienne Trixie Friganza wowed Jacksonville audiences in the star-billing spot); to conclude with an acrobatic troupe.*

Vaudeville continued entertaining the Jacksonville theatre patrons even when the silent movie was introduced to the area. According to Gould, they would show a movie to clear the theatre between shows, but things changed radically when "talkies" came to town. Gould said, "when the talkies came in, a proud tradition started to take its final bow."

Thankfully, the Palace Theatre, which was located on the southwest corner of Ocean and Forsyth Streets, adjusted to the changing times, and

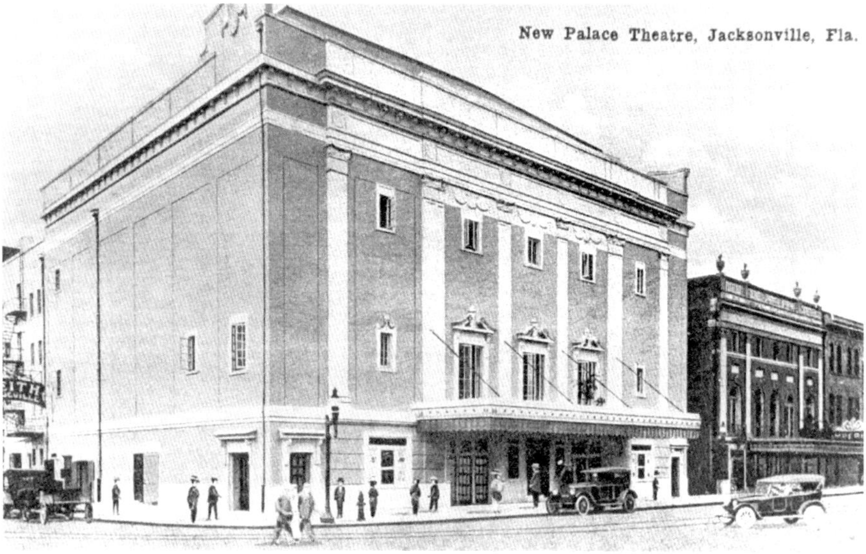

The Palace Theatre, early 1900s. *Courtesy of the Florida State Photographic Archives.*

View of theatres on Forsyth Street in Downtown Jacksonville, early 1900s. *Courtesy of the Florida State Photographic Archives.*

even though it had a full theatrical stage, its owners installed a screen so that these "new fangled talking moving pictures" could be shown to a fascinated public.

Circuit Court judge Frank H. Elmore served as an usher at the Palace on its opening night. In the piece that he wrote in the *Jacksonville Journal* on November 4, 1971, he told of many of the theatres in the city during his youth. He talked of the Rialto, which was first known as the Prince Theatre. He talked of the Savoy, the Lyric and the Orpheum, which was sometimes called the Airdome since it had an open roof. He spoke of the Duval Theatre, later known as the Temple.

But the saddest fact he revealed was that of the death of the Palace Theatre's manager, George H. Hickman, who was shot and killed on September 4, 1921, during a robbery by Frank Rollins and John H. Pope. It caused quite a sensational stir at the time.

The Palace did very well as it adjusted to silent movies, but the talkies made the theatre's survival difficult. In the '50s, the Palace was torn down to make room for a parking lot.

PARK OPERA HOUSE

I would be horribly remiss if I were to leave out the Park Opera House, even though no one living would be able to remember it. In an article published in the *Florida Times-Union* on November 28, 1948, James C. Craig said that the Park Theatre, more popularly called the Park Opera House, "was the amusement center of Jacksonville from 1885 until it was destroyed by the 1901 fire. It was located at the southeast corner of Duval and Laura Streets."

His article went on to say that on February 22, 1888, President Grover Cleveland had attended a minstrel show at the Park Opera House. It was called the "President's Reception," a parody of what was supposed to be going on across the street at the St. James Hotel, where the president was staying. Later that same year, the son of Charles Dickens would come and give a reading at the Park Opera House.

Sadly, the opera house was never rebuilt. The article ended saying that "none of the men and women who lived here in the 1890's is willing to accept a substitute for the place the Park Opera House has in their hearts."

Several decades later, Yvonne Parker, *Times-Union* special writer, wrote an article that was published on December 27, 1964. It said, "Jacksonville's first opera house was a converted roller skating rink and newspaper critics often suggested that it could use more heaters, but touring companies, warmed by ticket sales here, called it the best house on the Southern circuit."

Later in the article, Parker mentions that the site of the opera house had first been occupied by the Union Hotel, which burned down. Next came the St. James Skating Rink. In 1883, the skating rink began being used for "theatricals and improvised theatre," and in 1884, Hugh A. Young came to Jacksonville from Ohio and leased the lot to build a one-story building. (It is unclear if the roller rink was demolished.)

Then, on February 22, 1884, the Park Opera House opened with Minnie Hanks and her company in *Faust.*

On September 25, 1966, another article featured the Park Opera House. It was written by Sharon Gould for the *Times/Journal* Sunday magazine. Its focus seemed to be on the glamorous nature of its patrons. Her article said: "Chattering satined ladies and top-hatted gentleman stepped from carriages in front of the theatre on Duval Street in the fashionable district near the St. James Hotel and across Hemming Park from the Windsor."

Every person of any social standing, according to the article, had come to see Lillie Langtry. Gould said she had "swept into Jacksonville in 1888 and the town crowded to the Park Opera House to see the beautiful English society woman who had scandalized England a few years before by becoming an actress."

Gould ended her article with, "On this night, when the curtain fell and Lillie had taken her bows, the satin, beplumed and high-hatted theatre parties crossed the street to the elegant dining rooms of the St. James to review their night at the theatre. Perhaps they concluded, with the *Times-Union* reporter, that though Lillie was extraordinarily charming, Jacksonville had girls who were prettier."

Such a glowing account only makes me marvel at how human beings have long enjoyed their theatre experiences. The clothes and trappings might have changed, but the experience is still very much the same. No matter where in the world you go or where in time you might care to look, we love being swept up into the magic theatres provide.

ST. JOHNS THEATRE

One of the wonderful aspects of researching stories for books is coming in contact with the excellent writers who kept us informed in the newspapers. Dick Bussard of the *Jacksonville Journal* and Sharon Gould, Shirrel Rhoades and Anne Hyman of the *Florida Times-Union* were outstanding reporters, but one of my all-time favorite writers has to be Bill Foley of the *Florida*

Times-Union. His work was often historical in nature, but he was able to do something with history that most of my professors have been unable to do—make it really live and breathe.

His article about the closing of the St. Johns Theatre was so poignant that I cannot help feel remorse that I was never in one of its audiences. The theatre closed on September 18, 1960, and Bill Foley's piece about it in the *Times-Union* brought tears to my eyes.

He revealed that the theatre had only been open for nineteen years, so it never grew old. He said, "The St. Johns never had a chance to become a scruffy mockery of itself. It was never doomed to be a sad house of exploitation flicks such as the Florida, nor remain empty and boarded and hollow as the Imperial and Empress or, to this day, the old Arcade, last known as the Center."

The St. Johns opened on June 5, 1941, "when the British sank the *Bismarck*, when baseball's Lou Gehrig died of a disease named for him, when boxing's Max Schmeling was killed in the German invasion of Crete." He also said that the place had been "done in persimmon and magnolia in a time when the moving picture theatre could get away with that stuff."

Foley said that the St. Johns was the only downtown theatre that "postdated Prohibition and the Great Depression. It was one of the last of the great theatres that sparkled and glittered and shined and made the city a place to be after dark."

He also said the theatre had nine hundred seats—seven hundred on the ground floor and two hundred in the balcony. On the occasion of opening night, so many came that the line to get into the place "stretched around the block up Laura Street."

The first feature to play there was *The Great Lie*, starring Bette Davis, George Brent and Mary Astor, and such dignitaries as the mayor of Jacksonville (probably George C. Blume since John T. Alsop Jr. would not take office until June 20, 1941) and Albert Warner, the vice-president of Warner Brothers, were present. "Running marquee lights made the St. Johns the brightest spot on Forsyth, downtown's bustling white way of a time gone by."

When at last the time came to close the theatre to make room for the expansion of the Barnett Bank, *Ski Troop Arrack* and *Battle of Blood Island* were shown as a double feature on the closing night. And that was that.

A short news article ran in the *Florida Times-Union* on September 17, 1960, that the St. Johns Theatre would close "tomorrow and demolition of the building will begin within two weeks." And so the St. Johns went out with a sort of whimper, passing into oblivion as so many other wonderful theatres before it had done. Thankfully, Bill Foley had properly marked the passing of the St. Johns Theatre and placed it properly in posterity for us.

STRAND THEATRE

In the year 1969, the *Florida Times-Union* ran a photograph and brief news story about the demolition of an old theatre. The Strand Theatre, a once proud and ornate edifice that had opened in 1917 in the La Villa area of the city, was reduced to a sad pile of rubble. Only the proscenium arch remained in the photograph, and almost like the many actors who had tripped upon its stage, it seemed to be taking a final bow. At least, that was the way it looked to me.

So, with that being my initial piece of information concerning the Strand Theatre, I consulted a variety of people, and I was able to locate and speak with Richard McKissick. McKissick presently works for the City of Jacksonville in Special Services, and on a recent sunny June morning, he and I strolled through the streets of the once thriving La Villa area. I was trying to visualize the area referred to as the "Little Harlem of the South."

There had been many wonders in the La Villa area, including the Globe Theatre, which was on the lower level of the Clara White Mission. The cafeteria served as the auditorium of the theatre. Many pictures of musicians line the walls of the Mission in quiet tribute to their talents and to their having performed there.

The Ritz Theatre was but a few blocks away on Davis Street. But on this particular June morning, it was the location of the Strand Theatre that most interested me. So, McKissick and I set out to find it.

First, we walked from the Clara White Mission around to the back of the building to where McKissick had lived and grown up on Beaver Street. Along our way, we located the space where Brad's Café had been—the place that served the best sweet potato pie in the world. We continued down Ashley and passed the shell of a building that housed the Lanape Tavern and the Wynn Hotel. Farther down Ashley had been the Frolic and the Roosevelt Theatres, as well as the Knights of Pythias Hall where, in the '30s, Louis Armstrong and his band played. He and his band members stayed at the Wynn Hotel.

Finally, McKissick and I found ourselves standing silently at the corner of West Ashley and West Jefferson Streets. Here was the place where the

The Clara White Mission, where the Globe Theatre was once located. *Photograph by Dorothy Fletcher.*

Strand Theatre had stood proudly for over fifty years—a space now part of the campus of La Villa School of the Arts.

The Strand Theatre had been a vaudeville and movie house that showed silent movies and midnight shows. One of the acts that McKissick remembered was the Brown-skinned Models, a traveling group of beautiful women, and their show was for adults only. Other acts included Ethel Waters and the comedy singing group of Pigmeat Marcum and Butterbean and Suzie.

The Strand Theatre was a place that McKissick knew well. As a young teenager, he worked at the Strand, often putting up the advertising posters and promotional pictures along with all the other day-to-day operations—popping the popcorn, selling ice cream. He also went with the owners to put up flyers in the neighborhood to promote the shows that were to be presented at the Strand.

As we stood silently at the corner of West Ashley and West Jefferson Streets, I watched as McKissick's gaze grew distant, as if he were no longer with me. It was as if he had slipped into the past and could see things I could only imagine. For me, it was moving to witness his reverie—the good and the bad.

Racial segregation was the law of the land when McKissick was young, and it was racial segregation that had created this pocket of African American culture. According to a *Florida Times-Union* article written by Beau Halton and published on July 26, 1998, "Racial segregation, that barrier to unity among the populaces in Jacksonville and elsewhere nationwide,

The Strand Theatre. *Courtesy of the Ritz Theatre and Museum Photograph Collection.*

was the impetus behind the one-time success of La Villa's business and entertainment district. African-Americans couldn't go to mainstream places like the Florida Theatre, so Ashley Street evolved out of necessity."

But in an article written by Carol L. Lewis, staff writer of the *Florida Times-Union*, and published on November 9, 1986, McKissick himself was quoted as saying, "Integration helped to bring about the community's demise. Theatres and businesses closed because black residents started going downtown and patronizing other businesses where they couldn't go before."

He reiterated that notion when we were together that morning in June. What was wrong with our city created this haven for the African American community, and when our city made things right with integration, the decline of this area began—that and the expansion of Interstate 95.

But there was one thought McKissick wanted to share with me. He really loves this country because its one "redeeming factor is its continuous refinement of America"; as time passes, things get better and better. For a man who started his career as a manager of a theatre in a segregated part of Jacksonville, he has come a long way to work for the same city in its Special Services Department.

And what of the Strand Theatre? Even though it has long since gone away, I can still see it sparkle in the misty gaze of Richard McKissick's eyes.

2

LIVE PERFORMANCE THEATRES

Jacksonville has a very proud theatrical history, one that includes several long-standing theatre troupes and theatre buildings. As a result, in Jacksonville's earliest history, full theatrical stages were needed to present plays, ballets, minstrel shows, operas, concerts and vaudevillian acts.

All of the earlier theatres had complete stages with a curtain, proscenium arch, stage and wings. Until the advent of the moving picture, the theatres were all live performance theatres. And people of an earlier time period would have flocked to such places as the Metropolis, the Palace or the Dixie Theatres.

Nothing quite matches the experience of a live performance: that moment when a live actor draws an audience into a scene so completely that its members lose track of private realities and exist in the character's for a while. Or when a concert makes people forget their troubles for an evening. We are most fortunate to have some very special live performance theatres right here in River City. And many are still in operation today.

ALHAMBRA DINNER THEATRE

Most of us can only imagine the splendor of the audience and the sheer terror of the operators at the opening night of the Alhambra Dinner Theatre in 1967. Shirrel Rhoades's review written for the *Florida Times-Union* and published on December 15, 1967, was glowing. "Opening Night at the Alhambra Is a Posh Theatrical Banquet" the headline read; but not everything that night went smoothly.

At 8:30 p.m., the roast beef was still in the oven. Apparently things were not going very well in the kitchen. And the sound of hammers could still be heard backstage. Since there was no carpeting on the floors yet, chairs scraped and scuffed loudly. It seemed that the four hundred guests, who included Mayor Hans Tanzler and other dignitaries, were taking it all in stride. Rhoades said, "Vintage champagne flowed faster than a Lawrence Welk bubble-making machine. Compliments of the house on opening night."

The long wait was worth it. The night was a tremendous success, even though the play *Come Blow Your Horn* did not conclude until just before 1:00 a.m. Rhoades's review was most favorable to the first cast members ever to perform in the Alhambra Dinner Theatre: Reuben Safer, Trudy Fox, Chris Keogh, Chuck Cannon, Ila Jerom and Sydne Kalet. Rhoades said:

> *The timing of the actors was as precise as an Acutron watch, no lags, proper uptakes, no muffled lines in the midst of applause.*
>
> *Keogh displayed the timing with professional aplomb, adding a few Scooby-dooby doos to his role (which was played in the movie version by Frank Sinatra). Cannon, a mimic mindful of Jacksonville's Ken Fallen, mugs and shrugs and proves himself receptive to George Ballis' faultless direction—especially as he puffed on a cigarette waiting for his "first grown up date" to arrive from the apartment upstairs. Schafer could do no wrong.*
>
> Come Blow Your Horn *was a thoroughly professional affair, from the direction to the New York cast itself.*

Ted Johnson, a San Jose resident who is planning to spend his eightieth birthday parachuting out of a plane, was the founder, president and part owner of the Alhambra Dinner Theatre when it first opened. His time with the Alhambra lasted for the first ten years of the theatre's existence. He said that he "sort of burned out" since running a dinner theatre is an arduous kind of undertaking. He had to design it, build it, run it, promote it—and it was a 24/7 kind of job. He eventually went into television production making Winn-Dixie commercials.

In the mid-'60s, however, Johnson was opening dinner theatres in North Carolina and Virginia, and he had been looking for a new place to open one when he landed on Jacksonville. Johnson had fond memories of the north Florida area; he had graduated from the Bolles School in 1953, when the school was a military academy.

A still from *A Funny Thing Happened on the Way to the Forum* at the Alhambra Dinner Theatre, 1969. *Courtesy of Ted Johnson.*

Johnson approached his then employer Leon Simon about investing in a dinner theatre in Jacksonville. Simon was enthusiastic, especially when he learned that there was nothing like it in the area and research indicated that this would be a great place for such a theatre to thrive. So, they decided to go to Jacksonville to open a dinner theatre. They needed one thing, however: a liquor license. What Johnson then learned was that he had an uphill battle to fight.

In an article in the *Florida Times-Union* that ran on June 28, 1967, just a few months before the theatre was set to open, Reverend C.A. Bates, pastor of the Woodhaven Baptist Church, went all the way to the top, Governor Claude Kirk, asking the governor to veto a Duval County bill that granted a liquor license to the backers of the Manor Dinner Theatre, the working title of the Alhambra. The minister also presented the governor's aide with a petition containing some seven hundred names, mostly from the people in the Center Park residential area. The Jacksonville Baptist Association endorsed his visit.

The *Times-Union* article went on to say:

> *The Manor Dinner Theatre bill has been controversial since the introduction, principally because of the theatre site's proximity to the church and the new junior college.*
>
> *Supporters of the theater claim it is a cultural project as Broadway-type plays will be staged for patrons as they dine. The special license the backers seek, which must be endorsed by the Duval delegation, would provide that cocktails could be served with meals. No package goods could be sold.*

Barry Zisser, an attorney with Zisser Brown Nowlis and Cabrey, gave me some of the background concerning the start of the Alhambra. In 1965, Zisser not only was an attorney for the Duval delegation to the Florida legislature but also eventually came to represent Johnson in his procuring of a liquor license. As Zisser put it, that was how "the odyssey of the Alhambra Dinner Theatre and the friendship of these men have continued for the past forty-seven years."

It should be noted that Zisser is also one of only a handful of people who can honestly say that he attended both openings at the Alhambra. When there were problems in the kitchen on the 1967 opening, Zisser pitched right in and helped pour champagne for the waiting guests. When the Alhambra reopened on December 2, 2009, after it had gone dark for a period of several months because of financial problems, Zisser was asked to serve drinks again.

Thankfully, for those of us who love the Alhambra, a special liquor license was granted by the Florida legislature upon application and approval. By mid-July 1967, the petition drive had failed to change the outcome, and a liquor license was granted.

When at last all systems were "go," Johnson could then concentrate on the show. George Ballis was chosen as the theatre's director, and he went to New York City in search of six actors to fill the roles of the play *Come Blow Your Horn*. According to an article in the *Times/Journal* Sunday Magazine written by Shirrel Rhoades and published on December 12, 1967, more than 350 actors answered the "role call," which included a "sizable sampling from the old home town."

From those exciting, albeit tumultuous, beginnings, the Alhambra has continued to provide countless theatrical memories for many of us. When Ted Johnson and I got together to talk, he brought with him two huge scrapbooks filled with photographs, reviews and ads of plays that he produced during his time at the Alhambra. Some of the performers

Alhambra Dinner Theatre still featuring Lee Meredith in *Marriage Go Round*, 1980. *Courtesy of Ted Johnson.*

who emerged from the pages of the scrapbook were Mickey Rooney, Arte Johnson, Morgan Fairchild, Bob Crane and Dorothy Lamour, just to name a few. And Ted Johnson was very proud of the fact that the Alhambra was an Equity theatre and only hired actors who were part of the Actors Equity Association, a labor union.

Johnson also told me an incredible story of the night a bank robber was arrested after the play. It seems this "cultural criminal" made reservations on numerous occasions, but he kept changing the dates. When he finally showed up as a patron, so did the teller of the bank he had robbed. She recognized him immediately, and the management called the police. The police surrounded the theatre, and when the man walked out with the others, he was arrested.

As do most people of a certain generation, I also have my own Alhambra memories. When my husband, Hardy, and I were still dating, we went to see *Boeing, Boeing* with Lyle Waggoner in 1970. In one scene, one of the characters picks up the phone and, without even pretending to dial the phone, says, "Airport? I need to make a reservation." We can still

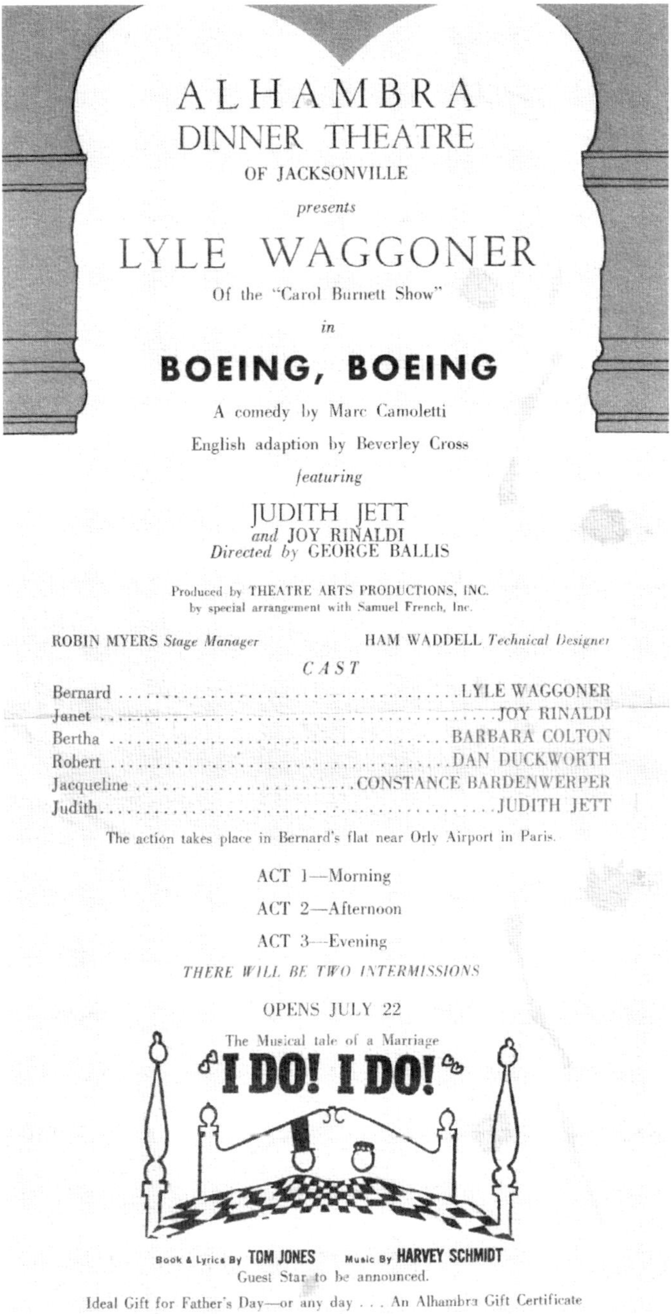

ALHAMBRA
DINNER THEATRE
OF JACKSONVILLE

presents

LYLE WAGGONER

Of the "Carol Burnett Show"

in

BOEING, BOEING

A comedy by Marc Camoletti

English adaption by Beverley Cross

featuring

JUDITH JETT
and JOY RINALDI
Directed by GEORGE BALLIS

Produced by THEATRE ARTS PRODUCTIONS, INC.
by special arrangement with Samuel French, Inc.

ROBIN MYERS *Stage Manager* HAM WADDELL *Technical Designer*

CAST

Bernard .... LYLE WAGGONER
Janet .... JOY RINALDI
Bertha .... BARBARA COLTON
Robert .... DAN DUCKWORTH
Jacqueline .... CONSTANCE BARDENWERPER
Judith .... JUDITH JETT

The action takes place in Bernard's flat near Orly Airport in Paris.

ACT 1—Morning

ACT 2—Afternoon

ACT 3—Evening

THERE WILL BE TWO INTERMISSIONS

OPENS JULY 22

The Musical tale of a Marriage

"I DO! I DO!"

Book & Lyrics By **TOM JONES** Music By **HARVEY SCHMIDT**

Guest Star to be announced.

Ideal Gift for Father's Day—or any day . . . An Alhambra Gift Certificate

Program for *Boeing, Boeing*, a play performed at the Alhambra that starred Lyle Waggoner, 1970. *Personal collection.*

laugh at that one. In 1982, when we were parents of very young children, we were able to sneak off and see *A Gentleman and a Scoundrel* with Jay Thomas, a local celebrity.

But the very best memory of my younger days at this theatre had little to do with the performances. I saw J.D. Salinger, the author of *The Catcher in the Rye*, in the lobby of the Alhambra Dinner Theatre. As an English major and an English teacher, I was struck speechless when I saw this literary giant so close that I could have reached out and touched him. He was dating Elaine Joyce at the time, and he had come to Florida to be with her during her run at the Alhambra in *6 Rms Riv Vu* in 1982.

As luck would have it, Gene Sweeney, photographer for the *Florida Times-Union*, happened to be there the same night as my husband and I when he took a picture of the couple. Sweeney was, however, forbidden

J.D. Salinger with Elaine Joyce at the Alhambra Dinner Theatre. This photograph was taken by Gene Sweeney Jr., 1982. *Courtesy of the Florida Times-Union.*

to publish the photograph of Salinger until Salinger's death, all part of Salinger's reclusive mystique.

On January 29, 2010, this very photograph taken in the lobby of the Alhambra Dinner Theatre ran in the *LA Times* announcing the death of Salinger. The caption on the *LA Times* website said: "Salinger joins actress Elaine Joyce to see her performance in '6 Rms Riv Vu' in Jacksonville, Fla. (Gene Sweeney Jr. / *Florida Times-Union*)."

Some months ago, I had a wonderful interview with Ham and Esta Waddell to talk about the Alhambra. Ham Waddell had been the Alhambra's set designer for over thirty years. Esta Waddell, his wife, is a retired educator for Duval County Schools. Both told me many interesting facts about the Alhambra.

Ham admitted that life for him at the Alhambra was a kind of blur. "Plays came and went so fast. The sets had to be changed so often. Every three weeks or so, I had a new show to prepare, and I felt like I was just pulling it off by the skin of my teeth."

Esta told me a great story about having dinner with Salinger. "He wasn't particularly nice, and he certainly wasn't very talkative. It was as if he were preoccupied, and I suppose he was—especially since he was there to be with Elaine Joyce."

Before the play closed, Esta was able to get the reclusive Salinger to sign a copy of *The Catcher in the Rye*. "Of course, he only signed my book with his initials, which meant that when I sold it, I could only get $1,500. I was told that if he had signed with his full signature, the book would have been worth $10,000. Oh, well."

Ham said that one of the highlights of his Alhambra days had to be when he was sent to get Betty Grable at the Jacksonville International Airport. Needless to say, he was thrilled. "Betty Grable was the top of everything!" he told me.

One of the most poignant stories I found about the Alhambra Dinner Theatre had to be about Betty Grable, the iconic pin-up girl of World War II and a top box office draw in the '40s. One night when she was performing at the Alhambra in 1973, she made it all the way to the dressing room before she collapsed after the curtain call. She, the consummate professional, had played through her pain rather than disappoint her fans. What no one at the theatre knew until then was that the fifty-six-year-old was gravely ill when she starred in *Born Yesterday* at the Alhambra Dinner Theatre in Jacksonville.

According to Tom McGee, the author of *The Girl with the Million Dollar Legs*, Betty Grable was given an injection of pain killers that night and sent to bed for a good night's rest. Then the next night, she went back on

Betty Grable and Ham Waddell at Jacksonville International Airport when she arrived to star in *Born Yesterday* at the Alhambra Dinner Theatre, 1973. *Courtesy of the* Florida Times-Union.

stage. And she continued playing her part for an additional three weeks of performances. After she had played at the Alhambra for a total of eight weeks to record-breaking, sold out audiences, she returned to Los Angeles, where she was taken to St. John's Hospital and surgery revealed that even though the lung cancer had had been arrested, cancer had appeared in her stomach. Within four months, Betty Grable would be gone. She died on July 2, 1973.

As the Alhambra was becoming quite a force in those early days, there was a young man in Chicago by the name of Tod Booth. He was the executive producer and director for the Drury Lane Theatres, and for ten years, he prepared "star packages" to play at the 147 Equity Dinner Theatres throughout the United States. (Today, only 5 Equity Dinner Theatres survive, and the Alhambra is the oldest.) His only dealings with the Alhambra in those days was receiving royalty checks from it. It wasn't until 1983, when he received a call from his agent, William Morris Agency, that his move down south began.

Claude Akins wanted to open a play at the Alhambra, since he had ties to Jacksonville. According to Booth, Akins was a spokesman for a bulletproof vest company located in Jacksonville. He could earn money for being in the play *I Ought to Be in Pictures* and then could earn more money promoting the vests in his spare time.

Booth's wife was to be the daughter of Akins's character, so the Booths came to Jacksonville. Tod was impressed, especially when they passed the Gator Bowl on the way to the theatre. He had just watched the game on TV the day before.

Booth really fell in love with the Alhambra, this "cute little theatre with such an intimate feel to it." He left his wife in Jacksonville for the duration of the play's run, and when he came back, he bought the theatre from Leon Simon (who had, sometime earlier, bought out Ted Johnson's share). Right there, in the center of the audience, a deal was forged and written up on a table napkin. The next day, the napkin was taken to a law office to be turned into a contract.

Life at the Alhambra was pretty smooth-sailing for twenty years. Of course, there were ups and downs, but a perfect storm was brewing on the horizon. It hit Booth full force in 2009. He said, "First, the economy tanked and the audiences began to get smaller. Then, they declared Beach Boulevard an evacuation route, and it had to be widened an extra lane. This meant that people couldn't see our sign from the road for all the construction, and it was difficult to get here. Then, since I had purchased some adjoining property and had borrowed money to do so, the bank I had borrowed from went under and called in my loan. They gave me ten days to pay up. I just couldn't go on."

Roger Bull, a reporter for the *Florida Times-Union*, announced on August 31, 2009, that the Alhambra Dinner Theatre was to "go dark." After being around for over forty years, the owners could no longer turn a profit since ticket sales had fallen off so drastically (155,000 tickets sold in 2001 to 85,000 tickets sold in 2008). Thankfully, Craig Smith, the current operator, came along. The *Times-Union* said that Craig Smith was "trying to buy the Alhambra and reopen it with improved facilities and dining. He said he was recruiting Matthew Medure, one of Jacksonville's leading restaurateurs, to take over food service.

"Smith said he'd then hire Tod Booth, the theater's current owner and director of most of its shows, to continue running the theater."

Craig Smith was good on his word. He and his partners bought the theatre and rejuvenated it, and on December 2, 2009, the Alhambra

Dinner Theatre came back to life, much to the joy of many people living in or near Jacksonville.

Smith grew up on the Westside, and he and his two brothers had rather typical American teenager experiences. Craig went to Moncrief Elementary and Stillwell Junior High, and he graduated from West Nassau High.

As he was growing up, Smith found himself at the movies often. He especially remembers going to the Murray Hill Theatre and the St. Johns on St. Johns Avenue, where he saw *Jaws*. He told of times when he and his buddies would sneak through a JEA water treatment easement to watch movies at the Fox Drive-in. He even saw *Grease* at the Blanding Drive-in.

One thing of which Smith is very proud is the stability of the Alhambra staff. According to Smith, three employees have been there for over thirty years, seven have more than twenty-five years and Becky Uibel has been there for twenty years. Such devotion speaks well of the entire experience at the Alhambra.

Becky Uibel, who graduated from Douglas Anderson School of the Arts in 1992 and who is the box office manager, is another person who related strongly to Betty Grable. Uibel was born in 1973, the same year in which Betty Grable died, so it was a no-brainer when she was offered a job at the Alhambra—she would jump at the chance to work there.

Uibel said, "Betty Grable had been a personal favorite of mine, so I just knew I had to work at the same place where Betty Grable had actually performed." And sure enough, Becky has been part of the magic. When the theatre closed in 2009, only to reopen under new management in December of the same year, Becky stayed for the "transition." During the renovations, she helped knock out a wall where double doors now stand. Inside the rubble she found a typewritten list of play suggestions for the 1979 season. There was also a price list from when the price of a ticket was only twelve dollars.

Even though the times and the prices have changed, much has improved. Craig comes out on stage before each performance and expresses his gratitude for the patronage of those who are there. Executive chef Dejuan Roy has replaced the rollout buffet table with an excellent to-choose-from menu of salads, entrées and desserts brought to patrons by servers. No one ever goes hungry. A night at the theatre is always satisfying, uplifting and joyful!

When I interviewed Smith, he said he believed that "it is the job of this theatre to enlighten and provide an escape for those in this community—those who might not get to travel to New York. For actors, my job is to be a stepping stone toward Broadway."

In either case, the Alhambra Dinner Theatre, past and present, is a crown jewel in the cultural life in the River City. The place has had its share of tribulations, as when we thought it had closed down in 2009. When it came back under new management, it was better than ever, and hopefully, we will enjoy many more performances and many more transformative memories.

FLORIDA THEATRE

When I went to interview Numa Saisselin, president of the Florida Theatre, I walked a long hallway to get to his office on the third floor of the Florida Theatre Building. On one side of me were offices, but on the wall opposite, there were hundreds of framed photographs of performers who had graced the stage of the Florida over the years. I suppose I was a bit awestruck in that I was hardly able to do the interview justice. My questions were not very penetrating or deep. Thankfully, Saisselin was warm and friendly. He immediately put me at ease, and then he handed me a most thorough document of the theatre's history that he had written in 2014.

Saisselin assured me that Jacksonville is very lucky still to have such a magnificent theatre as the Florida Theatre. "When the Florida Theatre was built, there were six theatres on Forsyth Street alone. When the Center Theatre collapsed in 2002, the Florida Theatre was the last theatre standing."

He then pointed out that thriving downtown areas of other cities—New York, Minneapolis, Cleveland and Pittsburg—have thriving theatre districts and that thriving theatre districts contribute to the viability of cities.

Probably more than any other entity downtown, the Florida Theatre has come to represent best what we have to offer the citizens of this place. It is our history, our culture and our pleasures all wrapped up in a beautiful, revered building.

According to the Saisselin history, it was in the summer of 1926 that construction began on the Florida Theatre on a site that had once held a police station. The building had been designed by R.E. Hall & Company of New York with Roy A. Benjamin as associate architect. (I had learned earlier in a *Florida Times-Union* article written by Bill Foley on June 10, 1999, that Benjamin had designed many important iconic buildings in Jacksonville, not the least of which was the 1935 Art Deco Elephant House at the Jacksonville Zoo.)

On that very subject, I received an e-mail from Debby Mizrahi Katz, who had a very strong connection to the architecture of the time.

> *Few people know that my father Ralph Mizrahi, graduated from the University of Florida, School of Architecture in 1934 and immediately joined the firm of Roy Benjamin Associates. Roy Benjamin had designed the Florida Theatre and had all the Florida contracts for the municipal buildings in the Twenties and Thirties and Forties in and around Jacksonville. My dad's first endeavors were the Elephant house, the San Marco Theatre, and Green Cove Springs Theatre. He also graduated with other architects, such as Kemp and Bunch, who started at Benjamin's and went on to open their own firm in the late '40s. They built the first insurance building in the Southside on the river, which was called the Prudential.*

George Fuller Company of New York was the general contractor of the Florida Theatre, and the estimated value of the building was $1.5 million. Michel Angelo Studios of Chicago provided the interior design of Mediterranean Revival style, and many of the furnishings came from Italy and France, including the Act Curtain, which required nine months for delivery since the design and fabric were French. The fringe was thirty-six inches high.

Florida Theatre employees lined up in front of the theatre in 1933. *Courtesy of Charlie Hillyer.*

Even though opening night would be six months before the first talking movie—*The Jazz Singer*, starring Al Jolson—would be released, the operators of the Florida were ready with technology and personnel that could accommodate this new art form. The new Florida Theatre offered audiences the best of both worlds—it could provide these "new" movies, but it could also provide live performances with its full theatrical stage. It also had a movable orchestra pit and a $100,000 Wurlitzer pipe organ.

Buddy Ross, who told me earlier about the Casino Theatre, shared with me one of his earliest memories, and it involved the Florida Theatre. He and his mother were in the audience one day, when all of a sudden, a spotlight fell upon a man and an organ rising up near the front.

"I think his name is Ed Knight or Ted Knight, something like that," Ross told me in his phone interview. "Words suddenly appeared with a bouncing ball, and everyone began to sing. I turned to my mother and said, 'Mom, look! That's magic!' and it really sort of was."

According to Saisselin's history, there were many organists who played for the Florida Theatre movies. Bob Mitchell was the organist on opening night.

Herbert Ruffner played the organ at the Florida Theatre in the early 1960s. *Courtesy of Ellen Ruffner Pierce.*

The next organists came in the following order: Lee Hamrick, Hal Stanton, Addie Berry, Jack Courtney and, finally, Jimmy Knight.

Jimmy Knight was quite the celebrity, it would seem. Ann Hyman of the *Florida Times-Union* wrote a wonderful tribute to the man when Jimmy Knight died at age eighty-two in 1992. Hyman called him the "dapper wizard who piloted the Florida Theatre's Mighty Wurlitzer through 1000 missions a year for 10 years." She also quoted many people who knew and loved the man. Jack Montgomery, who was Knight's friend and physician, said, "His knowledge of music was encyclopedic. He has been a hero of mine since I was a child and used to see him play at the Florida Theatre. He was sophisticated and charming and I never met anybody who didn't love him on sight."

Hyman also quoted Lee Turner, a Jacksonville musician who was one of Knight's music students in the early '70s. "I remember when I was small, going and seeing him rise up out of the pit with the great theatrical organ, with the spotlight on him. It was an exciting thing."

And Hyman also included a quote from Madge Bruer, music program director for WJCT-Stereo 90. "He [Knight] was a real important part of the city. Of course, he was kind of the maitre d' of the Mighty Wurlitzer, but it was more than that. He liked all sorts of things, all sorts of music. Organ music. Circus music. Classical music, and he liked baseball. He was a great Braves fan. He was a good friend. You always remember the originals."

I was given a rare glimpse into Knight's personality. I was allowed to look at a special letter written by Knight to his boss back home, Guy Kenimer. Knight was serving his country in North Africa in the artillery during World War II, and his letter to Kenimer is dated May 10, 1943. In it, he said:

> *I'm glad that Maurice is still pleasing the customers, but I still resent—can't help it—the idea of anyone playing "my" organ. It's funny how you get to feel about an instrument, and the old Arcade organ and the one in the Florida are very dear to me. I've been storing away a few ideas for solos when I get back, and am constantly on the alert for pop tunes which I think would interest the folks back home. I have three I know they'd be nuts about.*

Knight was writing this letter to Guy Kenimer, the first manager for the Florida Theatre. I was able to speak at length with his grandson Charlie Hillyer, a realtor who now lives in the Switzerland area. Hillyer provided me with many wonderful pieces of history concerning the Florida Theatre. Along with letters and photographs, there was a commemorative ticket key chain that was given to the first fifty patrons at the Florida's reopening after

Judy Garland and her mother, Ethel Marion Gumm, are seated. Guy A. Kenimer, the manager of the Florida Theatre, is standing behind Gumm, and an unidentified man stands behind Garland. Judy Garland had come to Jacksonville and the Florida Theatre to promote *The Wizard of Oz* in 1939 or '40. *Courtesy of Charlie Hillyer.*

its major renovation. One of the best pieces of memorabilia, however, was a photograph of Judy Garland, her mother and Guy Kenimer. Garland was in Jacksonville to promote her new movie *The Wizard of Oz*, which was playing at the Florida Theatre.

Hillyer was obviously quite proud of his grandfather's role in the history of Jacksonville, and after reading a different letter, written by Kenimer on

February 16, 1962, one can see that the man was quite accomplished. He was presenting his résumé to Claude L. Smith Jr., and he said:

> *I attended the Georgia School of Technology, after which I was employed in the engineering department of Southern Bell Telephone Company in Atlanta. Later I served in the infantry as a first lieutenant with the Sixth Division, with approximately one and a one-half years of overseas service.*
>
> *After the Armistice I returned to the states and joined the S.A. Lynch Theatre Enterprises, Atlanta, operators of approximately 800 theatres throughout the southeast. For them I managed a theatre on Peachtree Street until my transfer to Jacksonville in 1920. Throughout my theatre career I remained with the same operating company which changed from S.A. Lynch Enterprises to Paramount Publix Theatres Inc. to E.J. Sparks (Florida State Theatres), back to Paramount—a period of some thirty years.*
>
> *During this time my duties covered a wide range of assignments, beginning with the management of subsequent run theatres, then the manager of the Arcade which at that time was the leading motion picture theatre in Jacksonville. Next, I went to the Florida at the time of its opening where I remained for several years, serving both as theatre manager and supervisor of all local Florida State Theatres. Following this I was district manager of 36 theatres in the north Florida Area (Jacksonville to Tallahassee, Orlando, Stuart), subsequently becoming assistant general manager and general manager.*
>
> *My offices, or headquarters, over these years were always in Jacksonville. And my duties included actual management of the Palace Theatre as a vaudeville house, the old Temple as a road show house; and the Florida. For some years after its opening the Florida presented a combination program of band shows with three five acts and motion pictures. On occasion, the Florida was used for concerts, bands, ballets, road shows (SOUTH PACIFIC, OKLAHOMA, BALLET RUSSE), symphony orchestras, presentation of St. Johns Dinner Club programs, automobile shows, and the like.*

According to the Saisselin history, during the Depression, (and this would have been when Kenimer was manager), attendance dropped off and the theatre closed several times. Staff came up with many imaginative ideas to draw crowds. There was Screeno, a Bingo game on the big screen. There was Bank Night when ticket buyers could win a one-hundred-dollar prize. There was also the Happy Hearts Club, an event that provided toys for

Right: Guy A. Kenimer and his daughter, Hallie, on the streets of Jacksonville between 1945 and 1950. *Courtesy of Charlie Hillyer.*

Below: Electric cooking appliance demonstration at the Florida Theatre, 1949. *Courtesy of the Florida State Photographic Archives.*

underprivileged children during the holidays, which Kenimer had started at the Arcade and continued at the Florida.

Many times when people remember the Florida Theatre, they immediately think of Elvis Presley. That is probably because of the national coverage Jacksonville received in the iconic *Life* magazine dated August 27, 1956. The article headline read: "A Town All Worked Up." The article read:

> *When Elvis Presley played Jacksonville, Fla. last summer, his easily aroused fans ripped nearly all his clothes off. Memories of this visit and of Presley's growing notoriety stirred up civic leaders, and when the singer headed back to Jacksonville this month to play a two-night stand the city was ready for him. Juvenile Court Judge Marion Gooding had warrants prepared, charging Presley with impairing the morals of minors. The judge declared he would sign and serve them if Pressley repeated the torso-tossing spectacle of his earlier visits.*
>
> *"I don't do no dirty body movements," protested Presley. But he toned down his act noticeably and the judge took no further action. Neither this nor clergymen's denunciation of Presley dampened teenage enthusiasm, and his six performances were all sold out. Elvis left town richer in pocket and with the prayers of devout citizens following him.*

The article shows a picture of Baptist minister Robert Gray denouncing Elvis from the pulpit saying that Elvis had "achieved a new low in spiritual degeneracy. If he were offered salvation tonight, he would probably say, 'No thanks. I'm on top.'" A gathering at Trinity Baptist Church was shown praying for Elvis's salvation after Gray's speech.

Even so, approximately 2,200 people packed the theatre that first night, and Judge Gooding even allowed his daughters to attend.

Along with all those girls, there was a future mayor and his girlfriend in attendance. Jake Godbold, the mayor of Jacksonville from July 1979 to July 1987, was just a teenager when he and his future wife got to see Elvis at the Florida Theatre. He told me in a phone interview that that performance was one of the reasons he loved the Florida Theatre so much, and as fate would have it, he would be instrumental in its renovation.

The Saisselin history revealed that as time went on, television and the lure of suburban activities were drawing the audiences away from downtown Jacksonville and the Florida Theatre. By the late '60s, major movie events were not drawing the attendance that they needed to make ends meet. In the '70s, the place was really beginning to show its age, and at one time, fewer than half of the 1,900 seats were even functional. The theatre finally closed on May 8, 1980.

When Jake Godbold became mayor, the theatre was closed, and he told me that there was talk of tearing it down. Thankfully, many organizations and people came forward to promote the theatre's renovation. According to the Saisselin history, Mayor Jake Godbold used the renovation as a means to help downtown economic redevelopment. The city council, the Jacksonville delegation to the state legislature and the Arts Assembly of Jacksonville all came together. With a grant of $500,000 from the State of Florida, $350,000 from the City of Jacksonville Department of Housing and Urban Development Block grant and $150,000 in raised and borrowed funds, the Arts Assembly bought the Florida Theatre for $1 million. About this time, the building was able to procure a listing on the National Register of Historic Places. Then, there came an energetic capital campaign that was able to raise a total of $4,090,500 for renovations and start-up operating costs.

One of Godbold's fondest memories of his time as mayor was walking from his office to the Florida Theatre, sitting in the front row and eating his lunch while watching the painter, probably Howard Thayer, create the intricate designs near the stage.

An article about Thayer and his renovation efforts ran in the *Florida Times-Union* on October 3, 1983. He had been in the navy for ten years before and during World War II, and he had met his wife in Jacksonville when he was serving at NAS Jacksonville. After his service was concluded, he and his wife settled in Jacksonville, and he went back to his first love: painting. He studied with the muralist Harold Hilton, and after many projects, Thayer's work began to receive many awards and accolades.

According to the *Times-Union* article, "The committee of the Florida Theatre of the Performing Arts asked Thayer to help with the renovation of the theatre. He's been busy repainting, redoing and renewing the inside of the building."

After many months of hard work and effort on the part of many people, the theatre reopened. On October 2, 1983, Jonathan Rogers, staff writer at the *Times-Union*, declared, "Opening night rousing success: Florida Theatre opening a memorable event."

In his article, he said that all 1,978 of the seats were sold out at fifty dollars apiece. A dozen or so police officers were on duty, including two on horseback; television news crews were busy filming dignitaries; and "a 1 million-candlepower carbon arc searchlight blazed across the theatre's front and into the sky." Inside, after many "addresses, commemorations, thank-yous and welcomes," there was "a medley of organ music, backed by film clips of cinematic luminaries from Clark Gable to Liza Minnelli." There was a Cole Porter Revue called *Some Like It Cole*, and the London String Quintet performed works of Mozart, Dvorak and Scott Joplin. Finally, the "strongest part of the show rested on the sturdy shoulders of Vassar Clements, a legendary bluegrass-country/rock/jazz musician who filled the auditorium with pure sound and pure joy, from the opening number *Westport Drive* to his closing piece, *Orange Blossom Special*."

Jake Godbold told me, "There are two things in my time as mayor of which I am extremely proud. One was saving the Jacksonville Train Terminal and helping it become the Convention Center, and the other was helping to save the Florida Theatre."

It is sad that just a few days before the grand reopening, Guy Kenimer died. In the Saisselin history, it said:

> *His passing was noted in a Memoriam in the opening night program: "Guy Kenimer, who died on September 17, was manager of the Florida Theatre from its first opening in 1927 to his retirement in 1955 as General Manager of 36 Theatres across the state of Florida for the Florida State Theatres. Mr. Kenimer was of invaluable service to the Arts Assembly in preparing historical information for the Capital Campaign. Mr. Kenimer is in large part responsible for the nostalgia many Jacksonville residents feel toward the Florida Theatre."*

There are so many people who have wonderful memories of the Florida Theatre. One of the sweetest was written in an e-mail to me from by Deanna Moss Lissner, a Southside resident and a retired teacher. She said:

> *When I was a young girl, the Florida Theatre was a magical place for me. I went there as often as my family would take me or drop me off with friends (it was a safe thing to do back then). I would pretend that I was a princess and the theatre was my castle. I mostly loved walking up the red-carpeted staircase to the second floor…my castle was so big and beautiful.*
>
> *We would watch movies from the orchestra, which was the first floor, and there was the magnificent organ playing before the movie started. Often, the words to the music would appear on the screen and we would sing along, as the bouncing ball led us through the song. Shortly, the movie would begin, and we would be lost in the magic of the Florida Theatre.*

> *Now that I'm grown, I am no longer a princess and the Theatre is no longer my castle, but it still remains a very special place for me and is indeed a jewel for the city of Jacksonville.*
>
> *Thankfully, the Theatre was restored and regained its original splendor. We enjoy returning there when we can to attend one of many events it hosts and to revel in its beauty.*

Of course, there are many other memories of the Florida Theatre.

Judi Watson Frazier, a retired dental hygienist, was born and raised in Jacksonville, and to hear her tell it, she spent a lot of time at the Florida Theatre. As she recalls, her first experience there was watching *Gone with the Wind*, but one of her best moments was when she was one of a group of lucky souls who got to see the premiere of the Beatles' *A Hard Day's Night*. "I was able to keep my commemorative ticket somehow. And I have been careful of it ever since."

Frazier and I spoke at length over the phone about how her father cured her of horror movies. "He and my mother sat behind me and my sister when the family went to see *Hush, Hush Sweet Charlotte*, and when that head, or whatever, came rolling down the stairs, my father grabbed us and that was it! Never saw another movie like that again!"

Frazier also remembered that they had a child-sized toilet in the restroom that had apparently been up-sized when the renovations took place. She spent many wonderful hours at the Florida watching musicals like *The Music Man* or a whole host of beach party movies.

Arlyn Morrison Dockery, an Arlington resident, told me about her love for the Dave Clark Five. When their movie *Having a Wild Weekend* was playing at the Florida Theatre, she was able to procure some of the stills from one of the managers, and she graciously shared them with me.

When I spoke with Lorraine Pratt Nelson, a retired educator for the Duval County School System, she told me, "It was safe in those days to ride the bus to downtown. We got off at the corner before the Florida Theatre and would eat at the Krystal before going to the movie. Krystal hamburgers were ten cents back then!"

Another interesting fact I learned in researching the Florida Theatre is that it had a nursery. In a 1950 article in the *Florida Times-Union*, it said that Margaret Vogel had managed it since 1927. The nursery was located on the third floor and was for babies and children up to six years old.

Linda Evans Cornelio remembered the nursery, saying, "I have very happy memories of staying in the nursery when I was three to six years

"HAVING A WILD WEEKEND" in the Warner Bros. motion picture of the same title are The Dave Clark Five and Barbara Ferris, who star in the hide-and-seek, tongue-in-cheek comedy-thriller.opening ....at the ....Theatre. Running wild on the English beach are (L. to R.) Dave, Barbara, Mike Smith, Lenny Davidson, Denis Payton and Rick Huxley. Printed in U.S.A.

A still from the Florida Theatre, which featured the Dave Clark Five movie *Having a Wild Weekend* in 1965. *Courtesy of Arlyn Morrison Dockery.*

old. There were wonderful toys. The nursery attendant wore a white nurse's uniform and was very kind. I loved it there and never wanted to leave when my parents came to get me after the movie. Now, it is a bar, and my son sometimes works as a bartender in that room! He said there is still a bunny or something similar on the wall from the days it was a nursery!"

Reverend Chris Lawrence, who grew up at the beach but now lives in Mandarin, shared a wonderful memory he had of the Florida Theatre:

> *In the late '50s a full-length feature film about the Lone Ranger was shown at the Florida Theatre, and my dad took me to it, and we sat in the balcony. At the end of the film, Clayton Moore, the actor who played the Lone Ranger, made a personal on-stage appearance on his equally famous horse, Silver. At the end of his appearance, the Lone Ranger and Silver rode offstage and my dad grabbed my hand and whispered, "Quickly, come with me." He led me out onto the fire escape, where we saw the Lone Ranger and his horse exit the theatre door into an alley between buildings and ride off onto Bay Street.*

Diane Justice recalls the days when her mother worked at the Florida. "Some of my most fond childhood memories were spent there. I would go to work with my mom and back. I would spend my time playing in the balcony. I can still recall the smells and sounds. When I was older, I saw all the Beatles movies and would drink the orange drink from the little orange-shaped container."

D.H. Eaton, the author of the novel *The Osceola Community Club*, remembered a great story:

> *In past years, certain big-budget film favorites were re-released periodically. One such giant box office release was* The Wizard of Oz. *When I was very small, my mother filled her car with neighborhood youngsters* [and] *then transported the group to the Florida Theatre to view this classic. Unfortunately, soon after the film began to roll, when Elvira Gulch bicycled by Dorothy's farmhouse bedroom window, Miss Gulch cackling diabolically, her bicycle soon becoming a broomstick, I went to pieces with fear. My mom had to take me out into the lobby area and stay there with me until the movie had ended. Forced to wait through the entire film in order to return braver neighborhood youngsters to their respective homes, my mother learned that day that giant-sized witches weren't suitable viewing for terrified toddlers.*

Ellen Ruffner Pierce, a longtime resident of Jacksonville, shared her special connection to the Florida Theatre with me. In the '60s, her father was the manager at the Florida Theatre:

> *My father had played the organ at the Florida on occasion. That was quite a thrill for him because it was a huge organ. So, he was quite pleased when he got the job as manager in about 1965. By then, I was then old enough to be a candy girl for thirty-five cents an hour. We had to wear uniforms.*
>
> *Another thing I remember was getting kissed by an usher in one of the phone booths they had in the lobby. My father was not pleased when he found out. He probably didn't know I was smoking in the balcony either. When* The Dirty Dozen *was showing, there was an intermission, which most movies did not have, so I was upstairs watching. I'll never forget that I was in the balcony eating a hot dog and smoking a cigarette. They let you do that back then. Anyway, I could tell the intermission was coming, so I had to make a mad dash back to the counter to serve the rush that was certain to come.*

The Florida Theatre today. *Photograph by Dorothy Fletcher.*

Finally, she added, "My father's real pride and joy was working at the Florida Theatre…To begin with, he was a showman and probably wanted to be an actor. He stood at the door and greeted patrons as they came in, and he asked them if they enjoyed the show as they walked out. He just loved it!"

The Florida Theatre has recently procured a grant for $150,000, contingent on a local $75,000 match, according to an article written by David Bauerlein for the *Florida Times-Union* on April 9, 2015. Bauerlein said, "The focus of the restoration will be the terra-cotta designs that feature images of mermaids and griffins. In some places, the terra-cotta has already cracked, exposing steel rods and over time, it would only get worse."

Thankfully, we all seem to be on board with keeping this wonderful place around for many generations to come.

FRIDAY MUSICALE

I think it can safely be said that the Friday Musicale is the oldest continually operating performance organization in Jacksonville. The present bylaws of the organization say, "The purpose of Friday Musicale shall be to cultivate music as an essential art form in the lives of its members and the Greater Jacksonville community," and this the Friday Musicale has done very well for 125 years.

The 2013–2014 Yearbook of the Friday Musicale of Jacksonville, Florida says that in 1890, Mrs. Claudia L'Engle Adams invited into her home eleven musical friends for "weekly afternoon music study." These weekly afternoons evolved into the artistic organization that the Musicale is today.

Mrs. Eleanor H. King, who was past president from 1957 to 1959 and who just recently celebrated her 100th birthday, told me via telephone that the Friday Musicale was a place where married women could continue to perform the music that they learned in school.

"Everyone learned to play a musical instrument back in those days. Everyone took piano, at least, as long as the parents could stand the practicing."

King loved to perform in a variety of ways. She could dance (tap and ballet). When the Florida Theatre opened in 1927, she was there performing. When she was grown, she taught tap dance at the Florida State College for Women.

In the early days of the Friday Musicale, the members would play for one another, and then they might perform in recitals for the public. But it was a members-only group of female performers. As time went by, patrons of the arts began to attend, and then male performers were eventually allowed to perform.

From the in-home settings of musician friends, the musical club flourished until 1919, when the president, Mrs. S. Bryan Jennings, called a special meeting to consider a permanent home. They purchased Concordia Hall, a gymnasium at 645 Oak Street, for $5,500 on June 3, 1929. An opening performance was held in November after remodeling work had been done.

During the next sixty-six years, the Friday Musicale served the region by providing the finest of classical music presentations, as well as giving deserving local students scholarships for music lessons, summer music camps and music degrees at colleges.

Then, in 1995, the building that housed the Friday Musicale was destroyed by an arson fire, and it could have been the end of it had it not been for strong-willed members. Bob Phelps, *Times-Union* staff writer, said in an article he wrote on March 28, 1998, that Barbara Suddath and Mike McDowell headed up a two-year financial campaign to pay for a rebuilding project, costing about $650,000. Insurance provided $215,659 for the building and the contents, but the Musicale wanted much-needed upgrades. The previous building had been wooden framed with a brick façade, and it was to be

The Friday Musicale building today. *Photograph by Dorothy Fletcher.*

replaced with cement block with a stucco finish. The group also wanted to upgrade for handicap access; provide a sprinkler system inside and out; and put in a larger kitchen, a much-improved heating and air-conditioning system and a security system.

The Jacksonville City Council provided a $100,000 grant, and more than $400,000 was raised by private donations. A month before the reopening, a $50,000 Steinway concert grand piano was donated, and another used grand piano was being purchased at the time of the article's publication.

One of the most lasting contributions the Friday Musicale has made to the arts in the Jacksonville area is providing scholarships for deserving music students. The yearbook says, "For over fifty years through its Philanthropic Department, Friday Musicale has awarded music scholarships to graduating high school seniors from the Jacksonville area pursuing degrees in music. These four-year scholarships are awarded to instrumental and vocal students annually. A panel of three highly qualified judges chooses the best of the best and awards the scholarships."

All in all, what began as a small group of talented women became a commanding organization that continues to serve Jacksonville and all of us who love music.

JACKSONVILLE CIVIC AUDITORIUM

I began my search for information concerning the old Jacksonville Civic Auditorium by going to my high school scrapbook. I was one of many Duval County high school seniors who celebrated my baccalaureate service at the Civic Auditorium, and I just happened to have the program for mine.

The Civic Auditorium was a gigantic venue, as I recall, where many family members could be accommodated for the ceremony that was to be more solemn than a graduation ceremony. My baccalaureate was held in June 1968, and even though I was excited beyond all reason with the trappings of being a graduate, I was still awed by how vast the place seemed to be.

It had been only about six years prior that the $5 million Jacksonville Civic Auditorium was completed and dedicated on September 16, 1962. On that day, the *Florida Times-Union* ran several articles and an editorial. On the front page, there was a three-column-inch invitation to everyone to come to browse. The next day, a full article written by John R. Barry appeared, saying that city commissioner Claude Smith Jr. encouraged everyone to come. He said, "The public is not only invited but urged to come to attend the ceremonies."

The dedication program had many wonderful events. It began with the playing of "The Star-Spangled Banner" by the 581st Air Force Band, and then the colors were presented by Jacksonville Naval Air Station Color Guard.

Introductions were made by Mayor Haydon Burns, and Reverend Paul Hartsfield, president of the Ministerial Alliance, gave the invocation. "God Bless America" was sung by Thelma Baker of the 581st Air Force Band, and then followed many more introductions.

Rabbi Sydney M. Lefkowitz of the Jewish Temple said a prayer of dedication, and the dedicatory address was presented by John E. Mathews Jr., state senator–elect. Reverend M.J. Kelley, pastor of Immaculate Conception Catholic Church, provided a benediction, and the air force band presented a full concert.

After all that, anyone who wanted to could go on guided tours during an open house.

The day after the formal dedication, an article in the *Times-Union* also written by John R. Barry ran, saying basically that Jacksonville had finally taken its place "as an enlightened city in an enlightened civilization." He paraphrased John E. Mathews Jr., the main speaker at the dedication, saying "the block-long building which houses a large auditorium seating 3,200 and capable of the largest concerts and theatrical productions, as well as a 600 seat theatre and massive exhibition halls, is a fine edifice."

Program for the Wolfson High School Baccalaureate at the Civic Auditorium in 1968. *Personal collection.*

There was also an editorial written on the day of the dedication that extolled the wonder of the new acoustical quality that this new building provided that other venues did not. According to the editorial, "The local architectural firm of Kemp, Bunch and Jackson, designer of the building, employed a group of consultants specializing in acoustical design and sound reinforcement systems. The same Boston firm handled the Philharmonic Hall in New York's Lincoln Center for the Performing Arts, the $15.4 million home of the NY Philharmonic Symphony due to open next week."

The editorial went on to say that our beautiful and well-planned Civic Auditorium will make it so "the audience will hear an orchestra as one has never heard in Jacksonville before. Even the coughs will be clearer."

As I continued my research, I came across a playlist for one of the "Battle of the Bands" for April 19, 1963, held at the Civic Auditorium. As luck would have it, I recognized a band on that list—the Classics. I was very grateful to know D.H. Eaton through some of the writing groups of which I am a member, and she just happens to be married to Dr. Wally Eaton, the professor of cyber forensics at Florida State College–Jacksonville mentioned earlier who is also a founding member of the Classics, later known as the Classics IV.

The Eatons very graciously invited me to their home, where we all reminisced about bygone days—drinking cherry crème sodas as we did so. It was so sweet to be able to relive some of those experiences that led us to where we find ourselves today. At last, they showed me an actual copy of the program I had seen online.

D.H. said, "This was the program booklet I brought home from that event, and I was just fourteen years of age at that time. I adolescently scribbled the foolishness we teenage girls of those long-past days would write when 'in love' with a teenage boy. I had just met Wally two months before the Battle of the Bands event, so I was still in a frenzy of young love insanity."

Inside the program, five judges were listed: Linda Elder, Lithonia Rozier, Tommy Tucker, Buddy Roberts and Larry McKenzie. There were two masters of ceremony. Ken Fuller of WAPE, the Big Ape, and Ted Jones of WQTY. Twelve bands were listed, as were all of the members of each band.

Along with all of this information, D.H. had all of her "doodles" and handwritten notes in the margins. Thankfully, she wrote the list of winning finalists on the back page. They were 1) the Lemon Twisters, 2) Tiny and the Nobles, 3) the Twiliters, 4) the Midnighters and 5) the Rhythm Kings.

The Classics might not have placed that night, but they were the only band in this particular Battle of the Bands collection that actually gained any sort of national recognition. After they honed their skills in all manner of teen clubs—Westside Teen Club, Southside Teen Club, Riverside Garden Club, Southside Women's Club and Good Shepherd, just to name a few—the ever-changing group told a go-go club owner in Daytona that they had just finished a gig in Vegas (which was not true). Somehow, the boys landed the job at this new place, and they were discovered by Allen Diggs, a talent scout for Lowery Music in Atlanta.

Of course, the songs that most of us remember from the Classics IV are "Stormy," "Spooky," "Traces" and "Everyday with You Girl." And to think that on April 19, 1963, there was one band in that list of Battle of the Band contestants that was destined for a better reward than placing in the contest.

The Classics went on to appear on *American Bandstand* numerous times. They performed on *The Joey Bishop Show* and even *The Mike Douglas Show*. The only show they did not play was *The Ed Sullivan Show*, and that was because, as Wally told me, they never had a No. 1 hit. Their "Spooky" made it to No. 2 on the same week that "Love Is Blue" made it to No. 1 and stayed there for six weeks. Their "Stormy" made it to No. 2 the same week that "Heard It Through the Grapevine" made it to No. 1. Such is the way of the music industry.

Of course, there have been countless other kinds of performances in the Civic Auditorium, from the annual presentations of the Jacksonville Symphony and ballets like *The Nutcracker Suite* to rock operas like *Jesus Christ Superstar*, after which my son announced "Mom, that Jesus could wail!"

But there were still to be countless more performances held in this space by the St. Johns River. According to an information sheet provided by the Times-Union Center for the Performing Arts, it was in 1996 that the Civic Auditorium was renovated at a cost of $35 million and became the Times-Union Center for the Performing Arts. It now has three theatres seating 3,000, 1,800 and 600 patrons, respectively. It is home to the Jacksonville Symphony, which plays year-round in the Jacoby Symphony Hall, and the FSCJ Artist Series and the Ritz Chamber Players are its top promoters. It also has a new pipe organ.

When I think back to all the times I have gone to the Jacksonville Civic Auditorium or the Times-Union Center for the Performing Arts, I can honestly say I have been thoroughly entertained and uplifted. The monumental moments at the Civic Auditorium, including schools' baccalaureate ceremonies, heartthrob battles of the bands and a live performance of *Thomas, the Tank Engine* that thrilled my grandson, have all enriched my life, and I am ever so grateful!

JACKSONVILLE VETERAN'S MEMORIAL COLISEUM

It is a fact that I have attended at least thirty graduations in what was once called the Jacksonville Veteran's Memorial Coliseum. There was my own graduation, those of my siblings and my children and those of the many students I taught as a high school teacher.

But there are many other reasons I hold Jacksonville Veteran's Memorial Coliseum in high esteem. I went ice-skating there numerous times as a kid, I saw wrestling matches there and I attended many, many concerts within its walls. Who could ever forget Bob Dylan's gravelly voice in 1966? Or Elvis's visit here in 1972?

It all began around June 5, 1959, when the *Times-Union* ran an article and photograph showing a crane hoisting the first of thirty-two cantilever columns that would support the roof of the coliseum, built near the Gator Bowl. The article said that the general contractor was the Daniel Construction Company, and E.C. Pirtle was the superintendent of the project. The Daniels firm had won the bid at $3,853,633 in April but had delayed construction until June because of heavy rains. The architects for the coliseum were A. Eugene Cellar and George Ryad Fisher, and they designed the place to accommodate everything from the world's largest circus to a boxing match.

When the Jacksonville Veteran's Coliseum opened about a year and a half later, it had twelve thousand seats and a diameter of 312 feet. Its playing floor measured 115 by 205 feet. A *Times-Union* article that ran on November 24, 1960, announced: "Coliseum Dedication Set for Today." The article practically bragged that the new sports coliseum was "completely fire-proof and air-conditioned." It also had 3,000 feet of exhibition space for industrial shows and conventions. There were three entrances and ten ticket windows to "keep waiting to a minimum and an unusually wide concourse has been designed to handle large crowds easily. The entire building can be emptied in less than five minutes in an emergency."

The article said opening ceremonies would begin at 4:15 p.m. that day, which also happened to be Thanksgiving. The program was to begin with music by Robert E. Lee and Andrew Jackson High School bands. Mayor Hayden Burns would introduce the guests after an invocation by Reverend Robert J. Gisler of Snyder Memorial Methodist Church.

The dedicatory address was to be given by William H. Terry Sr. of Jacksonville, who was also a member of the Baseball Hall of Fame. The benediction would be provided by Rabbi Sidney M. Lefkowitz of Congregation Ahavath Chesed.

Program for Wolfson High School's graduation ceremony conducted in the Jacksonville Veteran's Memorial Coliseum in 1968. *Personal collection.*

Dave Clark Five news conference at the Roosevelt Hotel when they came to perform in the coliseum in 1965. *Courtesy of Arlyn Morrison Dockery.*

With such an august assembly, it only stands to reason that the coliseum would serve as an important center of entertainment in our city. Thankfully, there were people who helped make this possible. Sidney B. Drashin, promoter extraordinaire and part of Jet Set Enterprises, was one such person. He promoted some five thousand shows over a thirty year period, starting with the teen dances at the National Guard Armory and Riverside Women's Club and moving on to shows at the Gator Bowl and the coliseum.

"Some of the greats I have brought to Jacksonville are Elvis Presley, the Rolling Stones and Lynyrd Skynyrd. I really liked Lynyrd Skynyrd. But mostly, I got into the promotion business as a fluke. My parents wanted me to go into law school or take over the produce business, but I loved music, and I had to be part of it," said Drashin.

Drashin's love for the world of entertainment probably got started when he worked in the Catskills. And he would be the first to tell you how very lucky he was to have been part of such an exciting life. He is even writing his own book about all the fascinating people with whom he has worked and all the behind-the-scenes stories to which he was privy.

We all have great stories about our times at the coliseum. Lynne Bryan Doueck told me, "If you want to talk about live performances, I saw Ike & Tina Turner. Jethro Tull, twice. Emerson, Lake and Palmer; Edgar Winters and Johnny Winters; Ted Nugent; Mountain, twice; Rod Stewart and the Faces…saw Joe Cocker. Saw Alice Cooper, twice. Saw Iron Butterfly. Saw Black Sabbath. Saw Sly and the Family Stone. These were all at the coliseum."

D.H. Eaton, mentioned earlier, remembers very well the WAPE radio station's Fall Convention because of her connection to Wally Eaton, a founding member of the Classics, later known as the Classics IV:

> *In 1966 Capitol Records Los Angeles had released the Classics' first nationally promoted recording, a soft rock ballad titled "Pollyanna." Being one of the star acts on that year's roster of WAPE's pop music celebrities was a high for the local boys who had grown up yearning to someday be on stage performing at one of the radio station's music extravaganzas. Sonny and Cher were the "headliners" of the show, but the Classics, and their "Pollyanna," held their own nicely. They were thrilled to be pictured in the Florida Times-Union ads alongside the other rock-and-roll celebs.*
>
> *Before the show started, the four of the Classics band members and WAPE disc jockey Ken Fuller were walking in a hallway within the back recesses of the coliseum. Two emotionally charged teenage girls dashed up to them and boldly asked: "Are you SOMEBODY?"*

When it came time to demolish the Jacksonville Veteran's Memorial Coliseum, Dotty Curtis knew she had to have a memento of it. Curtis, a longtime Jacksonville resident now living in Arlington, was simply heartsick when the coliseum came tumbling down.

"From the very beginning, my husband and I had ties to the coliseum. So, I called the demolition company and said, 'I want some bricks from the coliseum!' The man I talked to was so sweet. I guess he thought I needed to build a big building because when I said I only needed eight or ten bricks, he laughed. I asked him when could I come to get them, and he said, 'No, Ma'am, I'll bring them to you.' And he did."

Of course, Dotty Curtis considers herself amazingly fortunate to have been part of the life of her husband, the professional wrestler Don Curtis. Any time she speaks of him, her eyes brighten and her voice takes on a joyful tone, and our interviews at the Beach Diner in Atlantic Beach covered many wonderful anecdotes about being part of the world of professional wrestling and the wonders of the coliseum.

Anyone living in Jacksonville during the '60s through the '70s is certain to remember that Thursday night was Wrestling Night at the coliseum. According to Curtis, at least 1,200 seats had standing reservations. There

Wrestler Dusty Rhodes at the coliseum. *Courtesy of Dotty Curtis.*

was a little old lady by the name of Frances Bellote who had a ringside seat on Thursdays in which no one had better try to sit! Even Mary Singleton, the first black woman to serve on Jacksonville's City Council (and who later served two terms in the Florida House of Representatives, as well as running for the post of lieutenant governor with running mate Claude Kirk), was a regular at the wrestling matches on Thursday nights. She and the Curtis family eventually became great friends, and Dotty and Don were often at Singletons' house for chicken necks and rice.

And everyone loved Don, if you were to ask Dotty. "Even Jake Godbold had wonderful things to say for his obituary."

When I looked up Don Curtis's obituary, written by Jessie-Lynne Kerr and published in the *Florida Times-Union* on March 8, 2008, there was a comment by Jake Godbold in it. The former mayor and the man who appointed Curtis chief of operations for the city's Recreation and Public Affairs Department in 1981 to oversee the coliseum, Civic Auditorium, Gator Bowl and Wolfson Baseball Park said, "Don was a true wrestler, not an actor. He was not only a great athlete, but a man of great character. I don't know of anything Don took on that he didn't do in a good manner. He had a good business sense and did an excellent job for us and commanded a great deal of respect."

Don Curtis was actually born Donald Bain Beitelman, but when he went to wrestle in Texas, he was informed that in Texas, people only had two-syllable names. He would thenceforth be called Don Curtis. (When their children were still young, the Beitelmans legally changed their name to Curtis). Thankfully, there would no longer be problems with ring announcers mispronouncing his name.

Curtis's love for wrestling began when he was captain of the wrestling team at the University of Buffalo. He then had a chance to work out with Lou Thesz, the world champion wrestler at the time. Curtis did well enough to commit to wrestling. It offered him a chance to see the world, and even though he had been asked to the training camp of the Baltimore Colts, he realized that he would not be able to support a family on the low salary defensive positions afforded to football athletes at the time.

According to his obituary, Curtis "became known for his finishing move, The Sleeper Hold." He was also well-known for his flying drop kick. The obituary went on to say, "He made his debut in Jacksonville in 1961 wrestling Hans Schmidt in the Coliseum less than a year after it opened."

According to his wife, Dotty, Curtis wrestled all over the state of Florida, traveling about one thousand miles a week, and they moved their family seven times in ten years. Eventually, Don Curtis was called to Jacksonville

From left to right: Jody Bryant, manager of the coliseum; Tommy Tucker, local celebrity announcer; Joe Louis, boxing champion and guest referee; and Don Curtis, wrestling promoter. They are standing in the behind-the-scenes corridor of the coliseum. *Courtesy of Dotty Curtis.*

to become a promoter for fourteen years. After promoting, Curtis was appointed by Jake Godbold to be the manager of the coliseum, which he did for about ten years. One thing of which he was very proud was serving as a role model for young men and being a volunteer wrestling coach at Bishop Kenny High School. Another honor was his getting to serve on the U.S. Olympic Wrestling Committee for the Munich Games in 1972.

The Jacksonville Veteran's Memorial Coliseum opened in 1960. *Courtesy of the Florida State Photographic Archives.*

It wasn't until Don Curtis died in 2008 that Dotty Curtis realized what a close-knit, caring society the wrestling community really was. "All of the wrestlers and their families rallied around me and my family. They still call to check on me."

It was a sad day for many of us when the coliseum was demolished to be replaced by the new arena (although, I must say that the Jacksonville Memorial Arena is lovely and much more acoustically accurate than was the old coliseum). Still, on June 26, 2003, the Jacksonville Veteran's Memorial Coliseum was imploded, and in a matter of seconds, all those ghosts of graduations, concerts, circuses, skating dates, monster truck events, rodeos and wrestling matches were swept into a new dimension—the corners of our minds.

And Dotty Curtis was kind enough to give me one of the bricks from the coliseum so I'd never forget the place (as if I could).

PLAYERS BY THE SEA

There is one theatre and theatre group that cannot be left out: Players by the Sea. Holly Gutshall, the dramaturge of the organization, provided me with

Present-day Players by the Sea Theatre on 106 Sixth Street. *Photograph by Dorothy Fletcher.*

an excellent history of the organization that said that the group formed in 1966 as a grass-roots art organization.

In 1972, the group received a gift of the old Beaches Theatre located at First Street and Fourth Avenue in Jacksonville Beach. It was the group's permanent home until an electrical fire leveled the place, and its members had to find a place to rent. In 1984, they set up shop in a former five-and-dime where they remained for the next fifteen years.

In 1999, the group was able to purchase a large building that had once been a laundry at 106 Sixth Street North. Members were able to create a 150-seat main auditorium, an 80-seat studio theatre, a large flexible classroom, a set building shop, dressing rooms, a storage area for costumes and props and offices.

In 2001, Players by the Sea hired its first executive director, Joseph Schwarz, and under his leadership, the organization continued to grow and prosper. The group added the Grune Family Gallery to showcase local art along with other improvements—enlarged offices, added dressing rooms and restrooms and increased staff.

Although it has grown dramatically (pardon the pun), it still maintains a "passion for creating transformative theatre experiences."

RITZ THEATRE

It must have been quite a day when the Ritz Theatre and Museum reopened in September 1999. According to an article written by Charlie Patton and published on Wednesday, September 22, in the *Florida Times-Union*, a ribbon was cut by Mayor John Delaney and other dignitaries. Then, the Edward Waters College Choir sang the "Negro national anthem," "Lift Every Voice and Sing," a song with lyrics written by James Weldon Johnson and music composed by his brother J. Rosamond Johnson.

The article continued by saying that Hurricane Floyd's passing by had delayed the work of hanging many of the exhibits, but even so, attendees "liked what they saw." The headline of the article seemed to indicate that feeling as well: "Ritz Opens to Raves; Museum Called African-American Cultural Center."

After this ceremony, there was to be a weekend filled with all manner of festivities: Friday there was to be a black-tie gala at $150 to $500 a ticket; Saturday there was to be a free street festival with a Jazz Show in the evening at $15 to $20 a ticket; and Sunday there was to be a cultural festival with a play entitled *The Colored Museum* performed that evening at $8 to $10 a ticket.

All of this celebration did not come easily. In the early 1970s, the Ritz Theatre closed and was boarded up. In the years that followed, it fell into a sad and dilapidated state. A *Florida Times-Union* article written by Carol L. Lewis and published on November 9, 1986, said that a grass-roots group called the Ritz Theatre District Inc., headed by twenty-year-old Anthonee Patterson, wanted to "maintain and restore the Ritz Theatre as a historical Jacksonville Landmark and to construct an entertainment and shopping complex that will make the city a showplace for the arts."

But in the eight years that followed, there would be "acrimony and false starts" according to an article written by Martin Wisckol in the *Florida Times-Union* and published on December 22, 1994. The headline announced "Ritz Theatre Dream Becoming a Reality." In the article, it said, "the Ritz board agreed to allow the city to assume ownership of the theatre and surrounding buildings for the purchase price of $426,000—and to oversee construction."

On February 10, 1996, an article by Steve Patterson in the *Florida Times-Union* said that construction would begin in the summer, and three years later, the grand reopening occurred.

The results are just magnificent, and a precious piece of Jacksonville's history has been saved to provide quality performances of all types—plays, reader's theatre and musical offerings. It is something about which we can all be proud.

Adonnica Toler, museum assistant at the Ritz Theatre and Museum, took me on a tour of the breathtaking complex that once was a movie theatre called the Ritz. Today, the outside of the complex is covered with Art Deco patterns and designs. The whole complex takes up an entire block. The lobby is spacious and lofty, and the theatre is state of the art. (I was thrilled to see a production of *Our Town* at the new Ritz Theatre during the Red Moon Theatre Festival on February 28, 2015.)

According to Toler, in its earlier days, the movie theatre, along with businesses, apartments and stores, stood on this block, and the place was very much a part of the social fabric of the African American community. The theatre opened in 1929 and was designed as a movie theatre only. It was quite a draw for neighborhood kids, who flocked there on Saturdays to enjoy serials, cartoons and full-length features.

Toler said, "Kids could get in with five or six RC Cola bottle tops or six cents for an all-day experience. If, however, any hadn't done their chores, kids knew there were some mothers who would come right on in and get their children right in front of everybody to take them home."

The present-day museum has an impressive art gallery called "Through Our Eyes" with works by local African American artists. There is a small

Employees of the Ritz Theatre, 1960s. *Courtesy of the Ritz Theatre and Museum Photograph Collection.*

theatre next to the gallery. In this theatre, a presentation of animatronics operates. Created by Sally Corp, the robotic show is called "Lift Every Voice and Sing." Here likenesses of James Weldon Johnson and his brother John Rosamond Johnson tell their life stories, which took place in Jacksonville and New York. And all of this is accompanied by music presenting songs written by the two.

Finally, there are many rooms depicting life in the La Villa area. There is a typical doctor's office, a store and a diner, but one of the most powerful

The Ritz Theatre today. *Photograph by Dorothy Fletcher.*

exhibits is that of E.L. Weems's photographs. Weems was the premier photographer of African American life and over fifty years created a considerable portfolio of work.

The Ritz has come a long way and has had many ups and downs in its history. With forward-thinking leaders and community support, the Ritz Theatre has been restored to its former glory, and I, for one, am grateful that the big red Ritz sign out front still sparkles like a beacon in the night.

THEATRE JACKSONVILLE/LITTLE THEATRE OF JACKSONVILLE

I think that of all the theatres I have attended, Theatre Jacksonville, once known as the Little Theatre of Jacksonville, has to be the most magical. It is in that space that the ordinary people I know in day-to-day life were able to change into completely different human beings, like the caterpillar to the butterfly. My French teacher at DuPont Junior/Senior High School performed in a mystery I attended at the Little Theatre, and I was shocked beyond words when he became a much more interesting man than the one I knew at school.

Both my daughter and my son attended Theatre Jacksonville Summer Camp in the late '80s, and I remember the warm glow only a mother can know when I watched in the dark audience the culminating performances of my children's summer.

Even my husband "got into the act" when he played the Belligerent-Man-in-the-Audience in the play *Our Town*. He was so commanding that the man sitting next to him tried to shush him so his daughter's performance would not be disrupted. And I cannot go any further without mentioning the mesmerizing performance of Robert Arleigh White, who was the Master of Ceremonies in *Cabaret*—such a miraculous transformation!

I suppose what I love so much about Theatre Jacksonville is that it requires me to be part of a game of pretend. I will, for the course of an evening, imagine that the people I know are new people, that they are allowing me to glimpse into their separate lives and become part of it. Thankfully, places like the Little Theatre/Theatre Jacksonville provide special opportunities to do this.

According to Sarah Boone, currently the executive director of Theatre Jacksonville, the organization known as the Little Theatre was a members-only

Interior of the Little Theatre, now Theatre Jacksonville, in 1953. *Courtesy of the Florida State Photographic Archives.*

group formed in 1919, and only the Friday Musicale is an older art organization in Jacksonville. In those days, one had to be a member of the Little Theatre in order to audition for a role in a play. In rare cases, auditions were allowed for someone famous or someone from a different location. The organization was run entirely by volunteers and even had archivists keeping detailed scrapbooks.

In 1969, the Little Theatre became Theatre Jacksonville and was incorporated as a not-for-profit organization. At that time, it adopted an open audition policy that is still in effect today. Theatre Jacksonville is not an Equity house. Its budget consists of grants, and only 16 percent of its revenue comes from the city.

Today, its mission statement says Theatre Jacksonville is here to "enrich lives and broaden cultural understanding through community participation in theatre arts."

Boone is a bit more practical. She thinks that her job is to "get the public to get off the sofa and come to the theatre," which is not easy in this age of multimedia wizardry. Boone has to be adept at using social media and ads to make theatre accessible to everyone.

Rehearsal at the Little Theatre, now Theatre Jacksonville, in 1961. *Courtesy of the Florida State Photographic Archives.*

Boone grew up in Avondale, attended the Bolles School and then earned a bachelor's degree in theatre at Florida State University. Her theatrical training then took her to New York City; Scotland; Washington, D.C.; and eventually back home to Jacksonville.

She has been able to put her talents to good use here. Many of the shows have a "Happily Red" format—her concert series that she created at Theatre Jacksonville. And she has been instrumental in keeping tickets affordable and providing an inclusive place for people to see theatre and be part of it. She said:

> *Theatre Jacksonville strives every day to touch the people of Jacksonville through the transformative power of the performing arts. Theatre brings the world home through live expression that entertains, educates and enriches our lives with stories of the human condition. We are extremely proud to provide a nurturing home for those who love to create fine theatre and those who love to experience it as patrons and audience members. As Theatre Jacksonville's executive director, it is thrilling to be part of this nearly century-old cultural treasure that's so vital to the artistic landscape of Jacksonville.*

Director Maurice Geoffrey conducting a rehearsal in 1961 in the Little Theatre, now Theatre Jacksonville. *Courtesy of the Florida State Photographic Archives.*

Theatre Jacksonville presents five plays a year; its Shakespeare at the Met has morphed into Classics in San Marco. It has gotten STEAM money to get Title 1 children in to see plays, and there are two summer camps and after-school classes.

The building in San Marco was built in 1938 on property donated by the Swisher family. At that time, it stood alone on the block and was not surrounded by businesses as it is today. According to the organization's

Theatre Jacksonville in 1953, when it was still called Little Theatre. *Courtesy of the Florida State Photographic Archives.*

website, the Theatre Jacksonville facility was placed on the National Register of Historic Places on July 11, 1991. Of course, this meant that even though it had been reincorporated as Theatre Jacksonville in 1969, it could not replace the Little Theatre sign with the new name. This was to comply with the register's codes.

Last summer, I had lunch with Robert Arleigh White at Uptown Market Springfield, and we talked about his tenure as the director of the Little Theatre, by then called Theatre Jacksonville.

From 1984 to 1990, Robert served at the pleasure of the theatre. During that time, he was also teaching at Samuel W. Wolfson Senior High School (1979–87) and at Duncan U. Fletcher Senior High School (1988–90).

When he became director of Theatre Jacksonville, his life started out as a kind of "freak show," especially when he realized how challenging the finances were going to be. The theatre had a budget of $100,000, an outstanding debt of $100,000 and two mortgages on the facility. Approximately sixteen thousand people attended performances that year.

When Robert Arleigh White left the position as director, the budget was $700,000, there was no debt and the mortgages had been paid in full with many endowments. Attendance had risen to fifty to sixty thousand patrons a year.

He related an interesting story about how the mortgages on the theatre got paid. The person who held both mortgages on the building told Bob one day that he needed money, so he was calling in the loans. Bob spent several sleepless nights trying to figure out a way to save the place, so he approached

Theatre Jacksonville today. The signage saying Little Theatre remained during renovations to maintain the National Register status. *Photograph by Dorothy Fletcher.*

Raymond Mason at the Atlantic National Bank. After some negotiating, an agreement was reached. Within minutes, Mason agreed to help, and White had the money to pay off the mortgages.

Harold K. "Bud" Smith, inventor of Swisher Sweets at the Edwards Cigar Company, approached White with a proposal. If the organization would name the building for him, he would create an endowment for the theatre. So, they agreed and Theatre Jacksonville is now housed in the Harold K. Smith Theatre.

Knowing the difficulties of running a theatre, we in Jacksonville are truly blessed to have such a wonderful group of volunteers who perform in a historic facility and who engage the community in all of that facility's plays and offerings.

3

MOVIE THEATRES

When I recall all the youthful hours I spent losing myself in the altered reality of theatres, I realize how rich my life has been. Specific places hold many magical memories for me. The Five Points Theatre is *2001: A Space Odyssey*. The Center Theatre is *Lawrence of Arabia*, and the San Marco Theatre is *Tom Jones.* Of course, there was more to the movie experience than just seeing the movies.

First, it was a time to dress up in our Sunday best and be as appealing to our boyfriends or girlfriends as we could be. Then, there was the taste of salty popcorn, and who can forget Jujubes, Dots, Milk Duds or Jordan Almonds all washed down with Coke or Pepsi or RC Cola? Going to the movies was a great pleasure for all of the senses.

Movie theatres were where we held hands, stole kisses or were scared out of our wits by movies like *Psycho* so that we could never take showers again. And it was to these places that our families took us when our hearts were broken and we needed to laugh out loud at the *Pink Panther* or *Cat Ballou.*

One reality that I encountered when doing research was that some theatres had very little written about them. The Arlington Theatre is one such example. I only located the Arlington Theatre in print when I was researching the Five Points Theatre. The Arlington was mentioned in passing by David Crumpler in the *Florida Times-Union* on November 5, 1984. He said, "River City Playhouse had been operating out of it [the Arlington Theatre] for two years when the theatre was sold and proposed new lease arrangements were unsuitable."

Betsy Bier, a former Arlington resident who now lives in Georgia, told me, "What I remember most about the Arlington Theatre has to be the ushers. They came down the aisle with their flashlights searching for those making out. And Jujubes. My mother would never get them for us at home, but she let us have them at the movies. I love Jujubes."

Bier also remembered the Town and Country Theatre, another Arlington theatre with little written about it. She said, "I think I saw a Tarzan movie there, but I am certain I saw *It's a Mad, Mad, Mad, Mad World* there. Of course, we also really thought we had arrived when a Dipper Dan Ice Cream Parlor moved in not far from the theatre, and I think there was a Tower's Hardware Store in the shopping center as well."

Another theatre about which not much was written was the Cedar Hills Theatre. Robyn G. Rathel remembered it, however. She said, "I remember as a young child going to a small movie theatre near the Cedar Hills Marina. They showed the scariest movies for this young girl. I remember going on my first date there (sixth grade-ish), and we watched *The Birds*, and I had to sleep for days with my cat as my protector."

If your favorite theatre is not mentioned in this section, it does not mean that it wasn't important. It means that few, if any, articles were written about it. After hours and hours of searching microfilms for elusive theatres, my eyes eventually gave out or I gave up. For this, I am sorry.

Thankfully, many other theatres are well-documented, and in Jacksonville, these provided sophisticated fare for us provincial folk—expanding our horizons in *Around the World in Eighty Days* or showing us a more sinister side of our fantasies with the movie *Blood Feast.* Yes, time spent in theatres was almost always positive and filled with marvelous fun.

ATLANTIC THEATRES/ROYAL PALM THEATRE/ NEPTUNE THEATRE

On April 4, 2007, the Atlantic Theatres in Atlantic Beach closed its doors as a theatre. This building started its life as the Royal Palm Theatre at the northeast corner of the intersection of Penman Road and Atlantic Boulevard. It had served as a comedy club and a film festival venue, but on April 5, 2007, it became a house of worship.

An article written by Drew Dixon, *Shorelines* staff writer, and published in the *Florida Times-Union* on April, 4, 2007, quoted the general manager

Exterior of the present-day Atlantic Theatres, once called the Royal Palms Theatre. Today, it is the location of the Beaches Vineyard Christian Fellowship. *Photograph by Dorothy Fletcher.*

of the Atlantic Theatres, Tom Fallon, as saying, "It was a bit of the twilight zone. I don't have a lot of that kind of experience where you are circling toward a final destination point…It's sort of like being in a whirlpool where you are going round and round and eventually you are going to be sucked into oblivion."

The theatre had been a live comedy club for several of its previous years. Since the 1,700-square-foot complex had a main stage and four smaller stages, it could easily accommodate a variety of crowd sizes and events. Keith Terry was literally the "last comic standing." Patrons paid a flat fee to get in that last night, and a cash bar was opened so that the staff could sell off inventory.

Then, at midnight, the complex closed as a theatre, and the following morning, Jacksonville Beach Vineyard Christian Fellowship held its first religious service in there.

Of course, there was an earlier, somewhat "infamous" event that caused an international stir at the Atlantic Theatres. In February 2007, workers had changed the wording on the marquee from *The Vagina Monologues* to *The Hoohaa Monologues*. A student group from Florida Coastal School of Law was presenting this play. Apparently, the marquee didn't sit well with somebody, although it is unclear who was upset.

There was also a period when the Atlantic Theatres ran surfing films each Tuesday night in March. The theatre became quite popular with surfers, but Josh Bolton, the organizer, felt that timing and lack of marketing resulted in a low turnout of about three hundred patrons over the four-week period.

It is somewhat comforting to realize that the Atlantic Theatres building still exists and has not been removed. If it can't be a theatre for movies or comics or off-beat plays, then it can serve in another capacity—that of providing space for a religious community. That has to be good for everyone.

On the southwest corner of the intersection of Penman and Atlantic Boulevard, the Neptune Theatre, part of Kent Theatres, showed movies and entertained beach citizens for many years. Betsy Fogg's father was Tommy Hyde, and he worked his entire career in theatres. He was fourteen or fifteen when he started and even worked, at one time, at the Beaches Theatre. He later managed the Neptune Theatre, where Betsy worked with her brother.

She said, "I was one of the best popcorn poppers around."

She also reiterated what I had been told by several others, that Fred Kent, of the Kent Theatres chain, was a great boss. He made quite a positive impression on those he employed. And the theatres on Atlantic Boulevard contributed greatly to the life of the beach community for many years.

There was one very uplifting Neptune Theatre story I was told by Reverend Chris Lawrence: "In 1977, shortly before I came to know Christ as the living, loving son of God and somehow God as well, I went to see *Star Wars* at the Neptune Theatre. I remember walking out of the theatre into the night and looking up to see a sky filled with stars and suddenly being overwhelmed with the thought 'Maybe there really *is* a force for good.' A few weeks later I met that force and was filled with him."

It would seem that sometimes movies can be more than just entertainment.

BEACH THEATRE

Imagine that it is Saturday, July 9, 1964, and you are at the old Beach Theatre on First Street in Jacksonville Beach. The lights dim, and when the movie starts, it is in a 16mm format with no soundtrack. A man named Bruce Brown stands on the stage and narrates as the footage rolls and dances across the screen. This is one of only two such public showing of footage that will later be used in his classic film feature *The Endless Summer*, an around-the-world odyssey of two surfers.

According to Johnny Woodhouse, associate editor of the *Beaches Leader*, in a May 2006 article, there were many surfing icons in the audience that night, having presumably come to be part of the Jacksonville Beach's first-ever surfing contest near the Jacksonville Beach Pier.

Mike Hynson wasn't the only big-name surfer in Jacksonville Beach that day. Also on hand at the contest and presumably at the Beach Theatre that night were Phil Edwards, credited as the first to ride and subsequently name "the Banzai Pipeline"; Joey Cabell, a Hawaiian surf legend who co-founded the Chart House restaurant chain in 1961; Hobie Alter, a tandem surfing champion whose catamaran design revolutionized sailing in the late 1960s; and Corky Carroll, then the Pacific Coast junior champion.

Billy Cato, a retired hardware store manager who presently lives in Douglas, Georgia, has his share of Beach Theatre memories. In the early '60s, Cato worked there as an usher, and that was his job on the night Bruce Brown was narrating his film:

> *As I recall it was mostly random bits of surfing stuff, but what I really remember most was what happened when Hurricane Dora hit Jacksonville Beach. All the beaches had been declared a disaster area, and the National Guard had been called out. Water was standing in the auditorium up to where the seats began to go down. It took forever for us to sweep the water out the exits.*
>
> *I also remember being in the ticket booth one day not long after the storm had hit. The National Guard had run me off one time already, but I had work to do, so I went back in the booth. About that time, President Lyndon Johnson rode by in his motorcade, since he had come to survey the damage, and he waved at me as he passed. That was something!*

Cato had many responsibilities during those days. Not only did he serve as an usher, but he also sold concessions and tickets and served as manager since he was often left there to take care of things on his own.

"Another thing I remember—I was the one who put up all the movie posters as the films came in. I put the smaller posters in the little five- by six-inch windows near the ticket booth, but I also put up a billboard-sized poster on the side of the building. It was made up of four to six large sections that I had to put up with a wheat paste. That was quite a job!"

Cato also remembers a historical tidbit that struck me as a bit odd. When the movie *Blood Feast* came to town, a registered nurse came along with the film. Apparently, the film was so shocking and intense that medical personnel were required to be on the premises in the event that someone fainted or had an "episode." It is hard to image such a thing today.

Billy Cato's sister, Judy Cato Pino, a retired system dispatcher for Beaches Energy, also got to work at the Beach Theatre. She mostly worked the concession stand:

> *I always had burns up and down my arms from reaching in to get the popcorn out of the popcorn machine. And I made a whole seventy-five cents an hour. I remember that the theatre's ladies' restroom had wicker chairs and a large mirror and a machine that sold Tangee Lipstick. I also remember times when you could bring a canned good and get into the theatre for free. Kids would be lined up around the block waiting to get in, holding their cans of beets or spinach—something they didn't want to eat at home.*
>
> *But one of my favorite memories occurred when I wasn't working. My best friend Mary Frances Weaver and I went to watch* A Summer Place *many times. We just loved that movie! Mary Frances and I did so many things together. Like we watched as they built the beaches pier. Of course, we had to be good wherever we went and whatever we did since my mother, Thelma Cato, ran a hair salon right across from the Wild Mouse at Griffin Amusement Park. My mother was hair dresser to all our teachers.*

The Beach Theatre has a long history. It opened on July 17, 1936, at the cost of $60,000, according to the *Ocean Beach Reporter*, and the eight-hundred-seat theatre featured four movies during its opening week.

The first movie to play there was *Private Number* with Robert Taylor and Loretta Young. The second was *Under Two Flags* with Robert Coleman, Claudette Colbert, Victor McLaglen and Rosalind Russell. *Showboat* with Irene Dunne, Allan Jones and Charles Winniger was the third film, and *Suns O' Guns* with Joe E. Brown and Joan Blondell rounded out the list.

Of course, during its long run, the theatre offered much more than just feature films. There were short subjects, newsreels, serials and cartoons. Betty Mann, currently living in New Smyrna Beach, was born in Mayport and lived most of her life in the Jacksonville beaches area. In an e-mail, she told me about what she remembers of the Beach Theatre most fondly:

> *Oh my! The Beach Theatre was where I spent almost every Saturday when I was about ten years old. Double feature, usually a Roy Rogers or Hopalong Cassidy. Two serials, lots of cartoons and the newsreel. A quarter would get you admission, a candy bar and a box of popcorn. Loved that place. I remember hearing about the end of World War II when our carpool driver picked us up after one trip there.*
>
> *Later we would go there at night with my parents. Admission was nine cents for children under twelve. Because I was so tall, my father paid the adult ticket price for me and caused me lots of grief when I went with friends and told them I was not yet twelve. Of course, the same cashiers worked most of the time.*
>
> *They did not sell any drinks when I was a kid, but I seem to remember in later years, your feet would stick to the floor.*

In a twist of fate that seems only possible in the movies, the Beach Theatre was badly damaged when an after-hours fire occurred in the building complex in which the theatre was located. On the front page of the August 26, 1964 issue of the *Beach News and Advertiser*, details of the fire read, "The blaze filled adjoining stores and the theatre with smoke, but left the rest of the building undamaged." The movie playing at the time was *What a Way to Go* with Robert Mitchum.

After that, the movie theatre was repaired and went back to normal. Somewhere between 1964 and 1972, the theatre went out of business. Then, according to a history provided by Holly Gutshall, dramaturge for Players by the Sea, the Beach Theatre was given in 1972 to Players by the Sea, and it became their first permanent home. A few years later, the building was lost to an electrical fire.

It is always sad when happy places come to sad endings. Everything comes to an end eventually, and so it was with the Beach Theatre. Still, the theatre takes its place in history, not only as a fun place to be for the kids on Saturday mornings but also as a place where cinematic history was made when Bruce Brown shared his surfing footage with an appreciative audience before his classic *Endless Summer* was even finished.

BRENTWOOD THEATRE

When former mayor Jake Godbold (who served from 1979 to 1987) was a little boy, there wasn't a theatre in his neighborhood until sometime during

Present-day Brentwood Branch Library, which was once the Brentwood Theatre. *Photograph by Dorothy Fletcher.*

World War II. Usually, he and his family would have to take buses uptown to theatres like the Capitol, which was at Eighth and Main Streets, or the Florida Theatre, which was on Forsyth Street.

In a phone interview, Godbold shared a vivid childhood memory he had concerning Jacksonville theatres. He said, "My mother and I went to the movies after we had gone to church one Sunday, and I remember that they interrupted the show to tell us the Japanese had just bombed Pearl Harbor. That was when I was a little fellow, and I will never forget that."

Godbold attended Jeb Stuart Junior High, and then he went on to attend Andrew Jackson Senior High. It was during his high school years that he landed a job as an usher at the Brentwood Theatre, which had been built in the early '40s in his area. Eventually, he became a doorman there.

"I have to admit that I had a lot of friends who'd show up at 10:00 p.m. when the box office was closed, and I would let them in. And it was really great to be able to cross the street in front of the theatre and go to an ice cream place, The Frosty, I think, and we'd get hot dogs and sodas there after the movies or after work. It was a busy little block for everyone on the Northside. We had a filling station nearby, and the church right there."

Dr. Wally Eaton had memories of his own of the Brentwood:

> *The Brentwood Theatre, on Pearl Street was located in the Northside neighborhood of my childhood days. I recall Saturday matinees included such cliffhangers as* Rocket Man *and other serialized films. Horror and science fiction movies caused us youngsters to be psychologically pulled into saving our planet from ghastly alien beings. Other films often shown in this theatre were cowboy movies, or westerns. These featured stars such as Lash LaRue, or Whip Wilson, along with Roy Rogers or Gene Autry.*

Thankfully, this theatre was saved from the wrecking ball. It was made into a branch of the Jacksonville Public Library System. It opened as a library on May 25, 1961, as Northside Branch in the remodeled theatre. This renovation replaced the earlier Springfield Branch, and it was renamed Brentwood in 1992. The interior was renovated in 2005 as part of the Better Jacksonville Plan.

As with all old "happening" places of our youth, it does my heart good to see buildings repurposed and saved. Thankfully, this was the fate of the Brentwood Theatre.

EDGEWOOD THEATRE

Michael Hull can tell you all about the Edgewood Theatre. All you need to do is ask. Hull used to help his father get copy ready for the *Breeze*, a weekly newspaper written for Westside neighborhoods. Hull, a Jacksonville native born in St. Vincent's Hospital and a retired civil servant, is a bit of an expert about the "goings on" in the Westside since he still has "the morgue" of the *Breeze* in full-sized volumes that take up the space a large refrigerator might. All the past neighborhood events and advertising for all the local shops sit in Hull's office keeping history preserved.

I asked him if he could talk to me about the theatres in the area, and without a pause, he told me all about the Edgewood located on U.S. 17 south of Edgewood Avenue.

"I used to have a friend who lived on Lakeshore Drive and I'd spend the night at his house and we would walk down the railroad tracks to the Edgewood Theatre on Saturdays," he said. "We would leave pennies all along the railroad tracks, and after the movies, we'd walk back to check to see what the trains might have done to them."

Hull went on to tell me how he could, for six RC Cola bottle tops or nineteen cents, get into the Edgewood Theatre, where he could see serial movies, cartoons, news reels and a Saturday matinee movie—all this while he and his friend ate Jujubes and Snowcaps and drank black cherry soft drinks that came out of a machine.

"I can remember how you'd put your money in, maybe a nickel, and a cup would come down a chute. Hopefully, the cup would come down straight before the seltzer and syrup came out. If not, you'd lose half the drink before you could get to it. There was even a sign nearby that warned patrons not to bother management about lost money in the machine."

There were other great features about going to the Edgewood, according to Hull. "They often held raffles for bikes—having a drawing with movie ticket stubs. They would get on the stage at Intermission and call out the winner."

It was also nice since the place was "air cooled," so kids could be there in comfort. The whole format was designed specifically for little kids. Even the patrol boys from Lackawanna Elementary School would redeem their tickets earned for doing well with their Saturday drills.

Perhaps Hull's favorite part of the whole experience was the movie serial. These short films had very exciting plots, and Captain Midnight and Zorro were just two Hull mentioned by name.

"I loved coming back every week to see how the hero would get out of a jam—like nearly falling off a cliff. Serials were the most exciting part of our movie time."

On April 24, 1988, Bill Foley of the *Florida Times-Union* published an article about the end of the Edgewood Theatre. He said that the Edgewood Theatre opened the same week that Gene Autry first kissed a woman in a movie called *Saddle Pals*. Actually, the kiss was given to Lynne Roberts, who was, at the time, disguised as his mother—hardly a romantic kiss, thank goodness.

These events (the kiss and theatre opening) occurred the Saturday before Easter 1947, according to Foley, and he went on to mention that the theatre building was designed by a "fledgling postwar architectural company of Kemp, Bunch and Jackson. Since that time, the company, now known as KBJ Architects, has designed much of the modern Jacksonville skyline. In a sense, the Edgewood theatre thus was the precursor to Independent Square, Bell South Tower, Prudential Plaza and other signature downtown buildings as well as to many Jacksonville families."

In the e-mail I received from Lynne Bryan Doueck, she told me that she often went to the Edgewood Theatre. She said:

> *We would go all the time in the summer for six RC bottle caps, which I got at the Colonial Foods Grocery Store. The assistant manager and manager were so nice! They knew my mother, a very good-looking woman, and since she purchased a lot of groceries for many mouths, they would go to the soda machine and dump out the caps for me to take home to pass out to the neighborhood kids. I saw all of the Frankie and Annette movies at the Edgewood. And I can still remember how the ushers tried really hard not to let you bring in outside candy.*

A *Jacksonville Journal* article, written by William E. Marden and published on October 1, 1984, quoted Kent Motes, vice-president of the Arms Corporation of Jacksonville, which had purchased the theatre in November of the previous year. He said, "The area had been in a decline since the [U.S. Highway] 17 overpass was built in about 1967." Apparently U.S. 17 or Roosevelt Boulevard had diverted most of the traffic from the area.

The article was initially written to announce the new uses to which the old theatre building was being put, and Motes had a good reason why his company was doing this reclamation project. He said, "What is it going to

Edgewood Theatres is now part of Jones College. This is a picture of the Westside campus. *Photograph by Dorothy Fletcher.*

take for people like ourselves who are developers to prove that old buildings are not only landmarks and interesting to keep around, but that they can be given new life and economic purpose so as to become part of the community."

The article said that where the theatre's concession stand had been there was now a title and mortgage company. Half of the building was to be used by the Arms Corporation of Jacksonville.

Today, the old Edgewood Theatre building is now part of Jones College. It has been totally revamped to included offices and classrooms, and its bright-blue roof and white walls are still welcoming.

EMPRESS THEATRE AND IMPERIAL THEATRE

It is interesting that whenever anyone mentions the Empress Theatre, he or she also mentions the Imperial Theatre. These two theatres were built at very different times in history, but they were very close together. The building that housed the Empress was originally built in 1901 and was a funeral parlor. Circuit judge Frank Elmore said in a *Jacksonville Journal* article dated November 11, 1971, that the Marcus Conant Funeral Parlor moved into the building after it was built in 1901. It wasn't until 1926 that it became a theatre. The Imperial opened in 1907.

Sadly, it was in this same article that the demolition of the Empress and the Imperial was mentioned. An earlier *Journal* article had shown a picture of what was left after the demolition had occurred, and the response from readers was surprising. It seems that these places were going to be missed since they had played a role in the youthful years of so many people.

One very blustery day in January, I met Ellen Ruffner Pierce for lunch at the Yum Yum Tree on the Southside. As we enjoyed our chicken salads, we took a trip back in time as she told me story after story about her father and all the incredible things in which he was involved.

Not only was Herbert Ruffner the organist at Skateland Roller Skating Rink on Kings Street, but he was also integrally involved in several of the movie theatres in Jacksonville. In the early '60s, he was manager for two theatres in Jacksonville—the Empress and the Imperial. Oddly enough, these theatres were right next door to each other on Forsyth Street, about two blocks from the Florida Theatre. Because they were together, Ruffner could easily manage the two of them simultaneously, which he did.

The Imperial Theatre, 1941. *Courtesy of the Florida State Photographic Archives.*

Ruffner was not of great stature, his daughter told me. "He actually wanted to be an usher, but he was too short for the job, so he became a manager. He really could stand up to people much bigger than he was. There were a lot of sailors who would come to the movies at the Empress and Imperial, and sometimes, they had been drinking. My father could handle them, though, whenever the need arose."

Ellen often joined her father at the theatres after school and after her skating practice was over. "I have a vivid memory of my sitting night after night in the Imperial watching *Circus of Horrors* in a room full of sailors while

Above: Interior of the Imperial Theatre, 1941. *Courtesy of the Florida State Photographic Archives.*

Right: Another interior photograph of the Imperial Theatre, 1941. *Courtesy of the Florida State Photographic Archives.*

I waited for my dad to count the money and do bookkeeping chores. Not a favorite time for me."

Buddy Ross, who spoke of the Casino Theatre earlier, has many memories concerning theatres in Jacksonville. When he was a little older, he would catch a ride on the bus to go see his dad, who would let him go to the Empress or the Imperial.

He said:

> *I couldn't afford the more up-scale Arcade, Palace or the Florida Theatres. They cost more since they got all the movies first. Things really picked up for us when the Riverside Theatre opened—it's called Five Points now. We would skate over there since it was closer to home than the others. Every once in a while, one of the girls would want to go with us, and we would let them skate over with us. We really liked being their protectors. It was really big stuff, you know.*

Whether a person went to either of these places because the prices were right or a person needed a ride home with her father, these two theatres were very much a part of the fabric of downtown for many decades. When they took these theatres down in November 1971, there a big hole opened in the heart of the city.

FAIRFAX THEATRE

As with many of the movie theatres in town, the Fairfax Theatre at 4122 Hershel is a treasured memory for many who grew up on the Westside—Ortega, Avondale, Lake Shore. It was a spend-all-your-Saturday-there kind of place complete with serials, shorts, newsreels and features. What I did not know myself about the Fairfax was that it also a theatrical venue—one with a proscenium arch. It was here that Richard Gainey got to perform when he was a kid. Gainey is presently an associate professor of multimedia journalism at Ohio Northern University, and at one time, he had worked as part of the floor crew at WTLV Channel 12.

"When I was a kid, I was part of the Children's Theatre at the Fairfax, and the Guild Junior Players performed there as well. I was in *Wait Until Dark* and *The Taming of the Shrew*," he told me over the phone. "In *The Taming of the Shrew*, the lead male actor was injured in a fencing scene—his

Present-day location of the Fairfax Theatre is now a group of businesses. *Photograph by Dorothy Fletcher.*

eye had been cut, and he couldn't go on the second night. There was no understudy, so I had to fill in as best I could, and that was something. We had script pages all over the stage and props for me to deliver the lines. That was indeed very scary!"

Still, this incident did not quench his love of theatre. "I had wanted to major in theatre, but there were too many rehearsals, and since I had to work my way through JU, I ended up going into journalism, where I didn't have to memorize anything."

Duncan and Tom Sawyer, both Jacksonville natives, invited me to their home so that we could discuss the theatres they knew growing up. The Fairfax Theatre was an important part of their lives.

Tom said, "The Fairfax—that little old thing—that was where we spent our Saturday mornings. We'd walk there, crossed the [Ortega] bridge and everything, and one of the best parts was the serial—the Roy Rogers episodes. Later, I used to love finding continuity errors in films—like the five hubcaps in *Bullitt.*"

Duncan Sawyer very generously drove me to several theatre spots, and the Fairfax building still stands and houses a group of businesses, now—a beauty salon and a dentist. We went inside and wandered the halls a while, trying to get the feel for the theatre, but its atmosphere had long since left the building.

We then drove past the place where the Cedar Hills Theatre once stood—now a parking lot—and we drove by the Lakeshore Theatre area and the Vystar Bank property, where Duncan said the Blanding Drive-in had once stood.

I sometimes wonder what younger people must think when they see teary-eyed older people looking at parking lots and new bank buildings as if they were searching for gold. What I think we are actually looking for is the fountain of youth, and all of those long-gone theatres represent just that to us people of an age. I have to admit that for me, it is certainly nice to connect in some part to a simpler, easier time of life.

FIVE POINTS THEATRE (RIVERSIDE THEATRE/ SUN-RAY CINEMA)

In the early days of June 2015, I stopped by one of my movie haunts to see if I could recapture the feelings that this once magnificent movie house used to instill in me. I tried to imagine myself young and excited to have a great movie experience ahead of me. When I walked in, I could see that the trappings were less elegant than I remembered. The artwork was far more modern and appropriate for a younger generation. But then, I came upon the stairs leading up to the lobby, and somewhere along the way, I met my younger self near the stairs leading to the balcony. That's when I felt at home.

Whether you know it as the Riverside Theatre, the Five Points Theatre or the Sun-Ray Cinema, the wonder of this place remains, even though it has had a rather roller-coaster history—some great heights of glory and some considerably difficult lows. But it has stood for over eighty-five years.

Always the trendsetter, the Riverside Theatre, began with groundbreaking technology, ready for the progress being made in the film industry. The theatre opened on March 12, 1927, with the silent film *Night of Love*, starring Ronald Coleman, but just a few months later, the Riverside Theatre screened *Don Juan*, starring John Barrymore with a new technology called Vitaphone. According to an article written on January 13, 1977, by Dick Bussard, city editor for the *Jacksonville Journal*, E.J. Sparks, the owner at the time, had spent an additional $20,000 of his own money, after the initial investment of $190,000 for the building, to install Vitaphone equipment.

In the article, Bussard had Bender (Dock) Cawthon, the projectionist of the Florida Theatre, explain how Vitaphone worked. Cawthon said Vitaphone was a disc, somewhat like a 33 1/3 record, that was perfectly synced with the film. There was only music and sound effects on this disc, and when Cawthon later used this technology at the Florida Theatre, streetcars rumbling by could throw the synchronization off. The only way to fix it was to start all over.

The film industry was still working on "sound on film" technology, which would not be available until the release of *The Jazz Singer*, starring Al Jolson, later in 1927, and even then, the film had limited words. There were only four songs and a few spoken words in this movie—like "Wait a minute, wait a minute! I tell yer, you ain't heard nothin' yet!"

Even so, *The Jazz Singer* was a huge financial success.

The article continued by saying that even though there were one thousand seats in the Riverside Theatre, the neighborhood was young and could not support the theatre. Sparks made arrangements with the Publix Theatre chain (which has nothing to do with the grocery business) to move the Vitaphone equipment to the Imperial Theatre downtown. By then, the Great Depression was making it difficult for any theatre to survive. So when the Depression was at its height, the Riverside Theatre had to close.

In the *Jacksonville Journal* article, there was also mention of a Jacksonville city councilman, M.C. Moore, who reopened the theatre as a second-run movie house. It functioned in this capacity throughout the rest of the Depression and through World War II. But, again, the business faltered. Not long after the end of the war, the theatre closed again.

Then, on August 11, 1949, an article ran in the *Florida Times-Union* with the headline "Five Points' New Theatre Open Tonight." It reported that the Five Points Theatre Corporation now owned and operated the newly remodeled theatre. Developer and rancher Bill Beck, who had several years of experience in theatre operations in Chicago, would be the manager. The opening film was *Too Late for Tears*, starring Lizabeth Scott and Dan Duryea.

The *Journal* article said when the new Five Points reopened, it was billed in its advertisements as "The South's Most Beautiful Theatre." The theatre now had nine hundred push-back seats, ninety-one of which were in a smoking lounge. Patrons could now enter from either Park Street or Margaret Street. Admission was fifty cents for adults, and it cost an extra dime to sit in the smoking area. Children's tickets were fourteen cents.

The *Times-Union* (1949) article about the reopening of theatre said there were two forty- by twenty-foot "black light" murals adorning the walls

A sign inside the Five Points Theatre around 1950. *Courtesy of the Florida State Photographic Archives.*

The marquee of the Five Points Theatre around 1950. *Courtesy of the Florida State Photographic Archives.*

representing a "Fantasia of Florida." Muralist Frank A. Lackner of Chicago had used a special florescent paint that made the murals glow brilliantly under black light when the house lights went down. It also said that the building was completely air-conditioned "for Summer and Winter comfort."

By the time I became aware of the Five Points Theatre, I was in high school. I remember seeing *The Graduate* with Dustin Hoffman and Anne Bancroft not long after I graduated. But the one movie that comes to mind every time I think of the Five Points Theatre has to be *2001: A Space Odyssey.* Just let me hear the first few measures of "The Blue Danube Waltz," and I am there!

One reason why *2001: A Space Odyssey* was such a treat for me, and everyone else, was this science fiction masterpiece, directed by Stanley Kubrick and based on a story by Arthur C. Clark, was filmed in Cinerama.

A *Florida Times-Union* article dated October 29, 1961, announced "Five Points Making Ready for Cinerama." Seven or eight years before the Kubrick film was made, the Five Points was reopening with this new cinematic technology. The article said:

> *Cinerama, which will be presented for the first time in this area when the Five Points reopens on November 15* [1961], *is a marvel of sound and visual engineering.*
>
> *According to those who have seen Cinerama, a startling illusion of reality is created by the process which is closely linked to the function of the retina of the eye and to the ear.*
>
> *The illusion is created by focusing the viewer's attention primarily at one particular object, with his field of vision encompassing everything on either side of it as far as the cornea of the eye can see.*
>
> *This is achieved by a wrap-around screen, now being installed at the Five Points, which is about six times the normal size for a theatre screen. The screen is almost a half circle—it is 146 degrees wide and 55 degrees high.*
>
> *The trick is in the camera, since no one single lens could cover the vast field without distortion; the Cinerama camera uses three lenses in making a picture each set at 45 degree angles. Each has a third of the picture's total width.*

I think seeing *2001: A Space Odyssey* in a Cinerama theatre made the experience all the more awesome for me. It was amazing!

On January 13, 1977, a *Florida Times-Union* news article headline said, "Landmark Theatre Closes Its Doors." The article said that Sheldon Mandell, the owner and manager from 1959 to the last day of the theatre in 1977, declined to comment, but sources within the film industry said, "Excessive cutthroat competition from suburban multi-screened theatres and other shady dealings in the industry were major factors in Mandell's decision to close down."

Again, the Five Points Theatre went dark, and after this point, the history gets a little murky. First, on May 21, 1984, a *Florida Times-Union* article written by David Crumpler announced that the River City Playhouse, formerly known as Open Theatre, was moving in to refurbish the theatre for productions like *Sweeney Todd* and *Amadeus.* It would open on November 5, 1984.

How long River City stayed is hard to determine, but an article written almost twenty years later by M.C. Moewe on September 1, 2004, in the *Florida Times-Union* indicated that Jack Shad and his brother Bill were working on a development project in the Five Points building. Jack Shad said, "This is a building that has been under-used and in bad shape…Everyone we've talked to about this project has been very excited about it."

Well, not everybody, it would seem. The article indicated that Club 5, a night club with a punk/metal reputation operating in the theatre portion of the complex was suing to remain in the building. The development plan, according to the article, was to convert the top two floors of the building into loft apartments, use lower floors for office space and make the ground floor for retail shops. They were planning to convert the old theatre section where Club 5 was into a restaurant, but Club 5 was suing, seeking to stay.

It isn't until June 26, 2007, that an article in the *Financial News and Daily Record* says that the Five Points Theatre and Historic Facility owned by the Mike Shad Company would be operating differently. Mike Shad said, "The theatre's been open for the past 15 months and has hosted a number of private events like wedding receptions and reunions. We've had a few public events as well, like an open performance by the River City Band. But this (show) is one of the first events to run consecutive nights since the theatre's opening."

Matt Soergel wrote an article for the *Florida Times-Union* on November 15, 2009, that talked about how the Five Points Theatre was trying to survive in a difficult show business world. The article said that they were going to try a new formula. A steady stream of first-run movies didn't work well because major studios insist their films run for weeks at a time. This is not a good thing for the single-screen theatres. So, as the article indicated, they were taking "the offbeat path."

On December 5, 2011, Matt Soergel wrote another article for the *Times-Union* that announced "Renovated 5 Points theatre to open this week as Sun-

Present-day Sun-Ray Cinema in the Five Points Theatre Building. *Photograph by Dorothy Fletcher.*

Ray Cinema." Tim Massett was now co-owner with his wife, Shana David-Massett, and even now, they seem to be making a pretty good go of it. At least, that's how it felt when I walked in a while back and imagined myself young and anticipating the first viewing of *2001: A Space Odyssey*.

MURRAY HILL THEATRE

On December 12, 1948, the *Florida Times-Union* ran a story with a headline that said, "Construction Is Started on New Murray Hill Theatre." The article included an architect's drawing as well as the details about the construction that had just begun the week earlier. It was to be located at the south side of Edgewood Avenue between Post Street and Jasmine Place. The cost of the one-thousand-seat theatre was $90,000, and the anticipated opening was to come in the summer of 1949.

Ben J. Phillips, a Murray Hill realtor, had the building constructed. H.S. Brownett was the contractor, and William H. Marshall designed the building. According to the article, the theatre was to be leased to a "well known Jacksonville operator, and that first run pictures will be shown."

The building was to be of a modern design and have fireproof construction, a mezzanine, the latest in motion picture technology and air conditioning. It would even provide a nursery where parents of children could see the movie from the nursery.

There had already been one glitch. According to the article, "The theatre is being erected as an addition to a store group. The part of the theatre to

Murray Hill Theatre, 1949. *Courtesy of the Florida State Photographic Archives.*

be used as the lobby was constructed at the time the stores were completed, but construction of the auditorium and the mezzanine was delayed because of building restrictions."

In any case, the theatre eventually opened in the early '50s, and Tom Tankersly, a retired educator for the Duval County School System, was there. "I was at the premiere, and I even remember the name of the movie that was playing that night. It was *Red River*, and it starred John Wayne. As I recall, there was even a place where mothers could take crying babies and still watch the movie. I sure loved the Murray Hill Theatre!"

And there were many things to love about this theatre. Tankersly said that he looked forward to every Saturday morning when a line of excited kids formed outside the Murray Hill. Inside, he and his buddies would sit through cartoons and double features in the cool atmosphere of an air-conditioned building.

"I remember that there was a five-and-dime nearby, and once or twice some kind of yo-yo expert was outside of the theatre doing all sorts of tricks. He almost always lured us to the store to buy Dunkin Yo-Yos at the end of the matinees."

Tankersly's father was a policeman, and he kept an eye out for the theatre. He would be the first person the managers would call if they needed help. Because he was so helpful, young Tankersly got into the theatre for free whenever he wanted. They even let Tankersly's father bring inside his dog, Punch, a boxer. Whenever his father watched a movie, the dog would lie quietly on the cool floor beside his master.

"When I was a kid," Tankersley said, "my friends and I lived up and down Edgewood Avenue. The drugstore, the dime store, the theatre, the bakery and the Dreamette—anything a kid could want was right there. It was a grand place to grow up!"

One balmy afternoon, I sat down at San Jose Country Club with Joy Atkins, who works as a grass-roots coordinator for State Farm Insurance. We watched as golfers, young and older, went about their classes and games. The weather was perfect for golf and for interviews.

Joy, who graduated from Lee in 1974, had the opportunity to work at the Murray Hill Theatre when she was in high school. She knew somebody who knew somebody, and soon she was working the box office, mostly. "It was the perfect job," she told me. "The theatre was only three blocks from my house, and after the initial rush for tickets was over, I could sit there and do my homework."

She remembers that movies like *Billy Jack* and the *Joe Cocker Concert* film were extremely popular. She also thought that there was a sort of rivalry between Murray Hill and the Edgewood Theatres since they had been a built about a year or so apart. Still, she had a good time recalling all the places close to the Murray Hill Theatre: the Edgewood Bakery up on another block of Edgewood Avenue and where she got her wedding cake, the Dreamette around the corner on Post Street, the Trade Winds down and across the street, a Krispy Kreme in an old brick building and the drugstore on the same block.

Then, she related a most memorable event that occurred while she was at work. "I was working the box office one afternoon, when a girl leaned up against a glass door. Suddenly, the door came undone and crashed to the hard tile floor. The girl was able to catch herself before the door hit the floor. We all watched as the door took one big bounce, and when it hit the second time, it shattered into a million little pieces. Thankfully, no one, not even the girl, was hurt."

Dianne Justice, another person with a powerful story about the Murray Hill Theatre, told me in an e-mail:

> *My friend Debbie and I went to the Murray Hill Theatre when we were about ten. My mom dropped us off, and she was to come back about 11:30 p.m. to pick us up. Needless to say, she and my stepdad fell asleep. We did not have a phone, and we had only a quarter left. Calls back then were a dime. We used the quarter and called Debbie's house. Her little sister answered and said she would walk across the street and let my parents know to pick us up. Instead, she went back to bed.*
>
> *We started walking, and you'd be surprised at how many people tried to pick up 2 little girls at midnight. My friend was a little more naïve and tired, so she was more willing than I to accept rides. I pulled her back every time. I was determined to get us home in one piece. We walked until we got to the Milligan's on McDuff and Beaver and to our relief, there sat my mom at the light. I will never forget that night. I grew up a little bit and learned not everyone has your best interest at heart.*

Today, the Murray Hill Theatre operates as a Christian rock venue that is alcohol free, drug free and smoke free. It is, according to its website, an "all-ages nightclub that showcases live music with a positive message." And it comforts me to know that another old theatre has found its place in the present of Jacksonville.

PLAZA ROCKING CHAIR THEATRE

In the early '70s, when Kevin Cordero was an upperclassman at Wolfson Senior High School, he had a job as an usher at the relatively new Plaza Rocking Chair Theatre located at Phillips Highway and Emerson.

The theatre had opened on January 14, 1967, according to the *Florida Times-Union*, and it was part of the Philips Highway Plaza Shopping Center as well as part of the Kent Theatres chain. The article read, "The newest indoor theatre in Jacksonville opened last night with a film on scouting in the great outdoors." The movie starred Fred MacMurray, and it was called *Follow Me Boys.*

Of course, Cordero wasn't yet there earning his $1.25-an-hour wage. It would be three years before he would be an usher who had to sweep up between movies with a broom and little dustpan that they gave him. Eventually, he would be trusted enough to be given the keys to open and close the theatre when the manager had other places to be. And there seemed to be no job he couldn't handle—selling candy and popcorn, selling and tearing tickets and manning the velvet ropes.

> *Yeah, I worked all sorts of jobs there, but the funniest thing I remember happening while I worked at the Plaza was when I heard Pat the projectionist yelling one night. I look up and this movie reel comes bouncing down the stairs with film flying everywhere. Pat had forgotten to secure the reel and when the reel was going about 600 rpm, it came loose and flew off and out of the projection room. There must have been fifty yards of film we had to get back on the reel.*

The Plaza was also a place where my husband, Hardy Fletcher, spent the summer of 1969 watching *Bandolero* starring Jimmy Stewart, Dean Martin, Raquel Welch and George Kennedy. My husband had been injured in an accident that occurred when a semi-truck hit the tollbooth he was manning on the Fuller Warren Toll Bridge. His arm was badly injured, and he had a long recovery period. Movies seemed to help him fill that difficult time. He and his only brother, David, would walk to the theatre every day, since he couldn't drive with his injured arm, and they watched *Bandolero* so many times that they eventually knew all the dialogue by heart. No family event ever passes without some bit of the *Bandolero* dialogue slipping out.

REGENCY ROCKING CHAIR THEATRE

On December 24, 1967, it was announced in the *Florida Times-Union* that on January 18, 1968, the Regency Theatre was to become the newest addition to the "$12 million dollar Regency Square Shopping Center." The 1,100-seat theatre was to be "a radical departure from traditional theatre design with the auditorium rising behind separate buildings housing ticket booths, concessions and offices. The auditorium was designed as a flat-roofed ovoid with continuously curving exterior walls. "Seating was to be the latest in rocking chair design."

On a spring morning, I spoke at length via telephone with Tom Smith, an Englewood graduate from the class of 1970, who as a teenager had been an employee at the Regency Rocking Chair Theatre. Smith, sixty-three and retired from the North Texas Tollway Authority, now lives in Irving, Texas.

He told me he started as a doorman in 1968 after having just returned from living in Arizona. Smith had run into a guy in the mall who was getting ready to quit his job at the theatre and who wondered if Smith would like to take his place.

He spoke with a man named Marty Sharon, who would be his boss, and soon, Smith was dressed in the theatre uniform—red sports coat with Florida State Theatres emblem, tie and shirt and blue slacks. He manned the door and served as a janitor and usher. It didn't take long before he was moved up to assistant manager, but occasionally, he still had to mow the lawn when his boss was dissatisfied with the work of the lawn service.

"I think I was one of the most popular guys in the school," Smith told me, "basically because I would give my friends free tickets."

When I asked him if he had any special moments, he said, "The very best moment I ever had at the theatre was the night my parents came to celebrate their anniversary. My father was in the navy and a big John Wayne fan, and *True Grit* was playing. I got them passes and set them up in great seats and had the usherettes bring them popcorn and sodas. My dad must have been really impressed because he said to me, 'You must really be important here to get this type of treatment!' That was nice."

One of the strangest things Smith had to live through was when *Midnight Cowboy* played at the Regency. The movie was X rated, and no one under eighteen was allowed in the theatre. That meant that all the young employees had to be temporarily laid off and a temporary adult staff had to be hired. "It was really awful," Smith said. "Many kids needed the job to make car payments and couldn't wait around for their job to come back, so many never returned. Then, when the movie had played its run, the temp staff left, and we had to go through a hiring frenzy to keep things going. That wasn't cool."

SAN MARCO THEATRE

The San Marco Theatre is a testament to flexibility. Since its opening night on June 5, 1938, it has reinvented itself many times. When the theatre first opened, it was a single-screen movie house, and its first film was, according to an article written by David Crumpler for the *Jacksonville Journal* (August 14, 1981), *A Slight Case of Murder*. It starred Edward G. Robinson and was billed as a gangster comedy. The admission was five cents.

In an article written to commemorate the seventy-fifth anniversary of the San Marco, Matt Soergel said in the *Florida Times-Union* on June 7, 2013, that architect Roy Benjamin had designed the Art Deco–styled San Marco Theatre. The San Marco had five hundred seats and no air conditioning when it opened. Unlike the other theatres mentioned, Soergel points out that only the San Marco has "been operating non-stop as a full time theatre, other than a few temporary closings for renovations."

On October 25, 1962, Judge May, a *Times-Union* special writer, announced in a headline, "San Marco Is Successful in Switching to Art Films." The article went on to say, "The San Marco Theatre is successfully making the transition from neighborhood movie house to one specializing in 'art' and foreign films."

Along with the change in format, there was a new sound system, new screen and curtain and new push-back seats. The first art/foreign film was *Only Two Can Play* with Peter Sellers, Mai Zetterling, Virginia Maskell and a small role for Richard Attenborough.

What I remember most about those "art" days happened when they screened *Tom Jones*. Someone, somewhere, wanted the movie banned. I was about twelve years old when this ribald movie came to the San Marco. Perhaps the tempest-in-a-teapot had only occurred in our circle of friends, or maybe it was more citywide. All I know for certain is that I was underage for the adult rating of the movie. My mother marched me right down to the San Marco in a show of independent thinking, I suppose, and we watched the movie together. I was sadly disappointed that the movie of eighteenth-century English hanky-panky was ridiculously tame. Obviously, the naysayers had not seen the film.

My favorite phase of the San Marco Theatre has to be its beer and wine phase. That phase apparently came after the *Rocky Horror Picture Show* phase—one that I was able to avoid completely. In an article entitled "Theatre Reopening," David Crumpler wrote in the *Jacksonville Journal* on August 14, 1981, that one hundred chairs had been replaced with small tables and that beer, wine and sandwiches would be served in the back of the San Marco Theatre.

According to the article, John Curington and Keith Kimbel, co-owners, had invested $125,000 to restore the old building. Showings of *The Rocky Horror Picture Show* had proved "disastrous to the condition of the theatre. Audiences have responded to the cult film by throwing food and paper and shooting water pistols."

Changes were made. No more cult-phenomenon moving pictures! There would be new tables, a new menu, a new sound system, a new and larger screen, new wallpaper and new carpeting.

David and Sue Blue, Mandarin residents, are presently the owners of the San Marco Theatre, and they enjoy a "very loyal following." Along with first run movies, they serve sodas, wine and beer and a menu of pizzas, nachos, quesadillas, hot dogs, paninis, popcorn and candy. David said, "It is a wonderful place to work. We hope to continue here for a long time."

Another nice touch is the huge old-time, Super Simplex 35mm projector that stands proudly in the lobby of the San Marco. It had at one time been the very projector used in the theatre. Now, the projector they use is digital, and movies can actually be started by David Blue's smart phone. My, how things have changed!

What hasn't changed are the feelings that this place still creates. I was surprised at how many stories people had to share about the San Marco Theatre. Sharon Danson Henley told me, "I remember one Saturday morning at the San Marco, when I participated in a hula hoop contest on stage. I won and received a gold hula hoop as a prize. I was extremely excited. It was hard to sit still during the movie that followed."

Linda Whipple remembered, "On Saturday mornings, my mom and other neighbor kids would load up and go to San Marco Theatre to watch cartoons and the early Disney movies. I saw *Bambi* there and remember crying at my first movie! Movies were twenty-five cents for like three hours of fun. We would get large bags of popcorn and all the kids would fight over it. Those really were the good ole days. I was about seven to eight years old then and 'in charge' of all the kids that went with us."

Rose Plotkin, a longtime resident of Jacksonville, wrote me in an e-mail, saying:

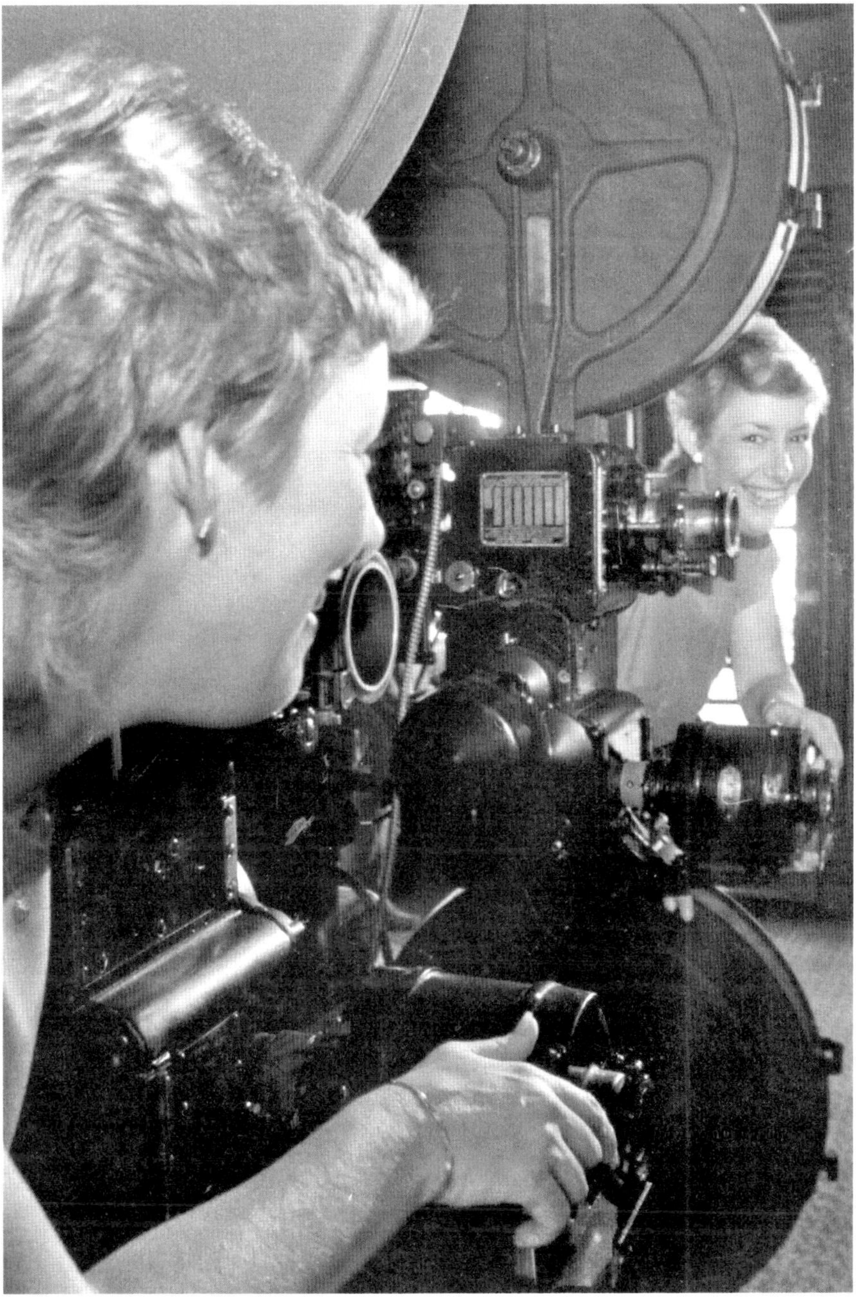

Claire Fleming King posing with the Super Simplex 35mm movie projector in the lobby of the San Marco Theatre, 1983. *Courtesy of Claire Fleming King.*

When I was about ten years old or so, the San Marco Theatre was the movie hangout for our age group. We would walk from our streets—Kingswood Road off Hendricks—to the theatre in a group of at least a half dozen. The price of admission was perhaps twenty-five cents, popcorn was a dime and the drink was a nickel. To us, this was a lot of money, so it was decided that the smallest girl would purchase a ticket that all of us had contributed to, and then, all but she would assemble at the back door. Magically, the door would open up, and we quickly sneaked in and saw the picture "at the reduced price." This was, indeed, a bargain because in addition to the main feature, we were always privileged to see the Movietone News, the coming attraction previews, the cartoons and the short subjects. If the movie was really good, we might stay and see it again making sure we got home in time for our curfew. That was our Saturday experience and our closest brush with the law.

Debby Mizrahi Katz, another Jacksonville resident, shared her San Marco story with me in an e-mail. She said:

The San Marco Theatre, was different inside than it is now. It had rows of chairs with padded seats and great popcorn and a candy counter. I think

San Marco Theatre today. *Photograph by Dorothy Fletcher.*

> *for children the entry fee was ten cents and adults' cost twenty-five cents. It was used as movie entertainment for most, but my mother would use it as a babysitter. When she had something like playing cards, Mahjong or meetings to attend, she would drop me off to see a movie, which gave her a couple hours of free time to do her activities.*
>
> *As a teenager I would meet my friends and we would go to shows on the weekends, usually we went to eat lunch at a restaurant downtown—Krystal's or Leb's—and then to the Florida Theatre to see a movie. Most Sunday afternoons, we would meet and go to the San Marco Theatre—only if the movies were age appropriate.*
>
> *I remember on Wednesday, the San Marco would run what they called an Art show; it was really a showing of a foreign films that usually had subtitles, and they were not usually age appropriate. Kids under thirteen were not allowed to attend that day.*

Today, the San Marco still operates much as it has for over seventy-six years. Whether you graduated from Landon long ago or are a new resident to the San Marco area, this spot in the neighborhood still beckons and still entertains.

4

DRIVE-IN THEATRES

It was sometime in the late 1930s that the drive-in movies were introduced to America, and before we knew it, there was a whole new way to watch a show. By driving but a few short miles, we could enjoy the movies in the comfort of our cars. With the window speaker providing the sound and a distant three-storied screen providing the images, we could chow down on treats provided at the concession house toward the back of the complex as we watched movies.

Drive-ins, as the name would indicate, were a creations spun off from American "car culture." As the automobile became accessible to more of the middle class, so were those things that catered to those driving the cars. One could drive up to a restaurant, order from a little box and have a meal delivered to the car. There were places to which you could drive up and get your milk and butter and eggs and still others where you could drive up to buy miniatures of alcoholic beverages and cups of ice. It wasn't long before some realized that when the sun went down, cars could gather on a field, and drivers could park and watch movies projected on a white building.

Many of us of an age can remember the joy when a parent announced that the family was going to the drive-in. It meant that first we could play on a playground right under the screen, and then when the sun went down, we could settle in the car with popcorn and candy to watch a show. Sometimes, we wore pajamas and fell asleep before we could finish the feature. Mom and Dad would carry us home and tuck us into bed still sleeping.

When we became teenagers and got to borrow the car for the evening, a whole new drive-in experience awaited. We could go with our friends to check out the opposite sex and sometimes we went with our sweethearts to enjoy a little privacy in the darkness. Many of us wonder why such wonderful places as drive-ins went out of existence, but we conveniently forget that it could be very hot in the summer or that the mosquitoes were always ravenous. It is no wonder that we slowly adopted the more comfortable spots on living room sofas to watch movies on TV.

Sometimes, what looks like the obvious cause of an occurrence may not be all there is to know about it. In February 2015, Rick Cohen was involved in a drive-in awareness walk that was to take him from Orlando, Florida, to Buffalo, New York. Sadly, he only made it to Beaufort, South Carolina, before a sprained ankle forced him to stop.

He was hoping to bring awareness to many rural, family-operated drive-ins that are being put out of business because they cannot afford the $35,000 upgrade needed to show digitized movies. On his walk, Cohen raised about $6,000 to help save certain drive-ins that still exist in Georgia.

Cohen, when he is not taking drive-in awareness walks, operates a thriving four-screened drive-in theatre in Buffalo, New York, called the Transit. Not only do its four screens allow many varieties of movies, but it also has a miniature golf course that adds another attraction to get people into the complex. His seasonal business runs from March to November, since it is too cold to operate a drive-in during the winter.

When I spoke with Cohen via telephone, his love of the drive-in was quite evident. When I told him my theory concerning the demise of drive-ins, he said, "What usually happened was the property upon which the drive-in was built becomes too valuable to keep as a drive-in. Drive-ins built inside the beltway were standing on land that was needed for residential development or commercial concerns. It was not a good business decision to keep that land tied up as a drive-in which was not used during the day and could not really bring in enough money at night to justify its existence." And I thought it was because of mosquitoes!

It really doesn't matter why, though. Those wonderful drive-in experiences live mostly in the memory of my generation. They are little gems in time that the latest generation cannot fully appreciate with their Netflix and HBO. Still, I cannot help but feel a special sense of wonder when the sun gets to a certain place in the sky and reminds me of when my father called us home early so the family could go to the drive-in. And sometimes that time of day makes me remember a special person whose invitation to the drive-in made my heart flutter.

AIR BASE DRIVE-IN THEATRE

Not many people remember this drive-in, at least not many of the people I have asked about it. All I could find about it was an announcement in the *Florida Times-Union* on September 4, 1948. The headline read, "New Drive In Theatre Opens," and the staff had provided a photograph, which looked more like an architect's rendering. The paragraph-long article said that the drive-in would be located south of the Naval Air Station's main entrance on Highway 17. The article said that the theatre had a five-hundred-car capacity and that it would show "currently released films from all the major motion picture producers."

Right next to the image of the theatre was another news article. It was more descriptive, saying, "Designed in a modern colonial motif, with the screen facing away from the road, the theatre has a capacity of 500 automobiles. The latest in RCA sound equipment has been installed, and a refreshment stand will be operated in conjunction with the enterprise. Plans call for extensive landscaping to be completed soon, making the theatre one of the most beautiful in the South."

As I kept looking for more information, I found a few ads for this drive-in. Michael Hull, whose family owned and operated the *Breeze*, provided me with an advertisement for the Air Base Drive-in. The feature in 1949 was *Big Calibre*, starring Bob Steele, and there were cartoons. On Sunday, the feature was to be *It Happened in New Orleans*, starring Rochester and Charles Butterworth. It was only thirty-five cents a person, and children under twelve got in free.

I found two very different ads that ran in old newspapers I had saved myself. The first ran in the *Florida Times-Union* on November 24, 1963, two days after John F. Kennedy was assassinated. It announced that *PT 109* with Cliff Robertson starring as a young JFK would be playing at the Air Base.

The second ad ran in the *Jacksonville Journal* on June 5, 1968, the day that Robert Kennedy was shot. The ad announced that it was $1.25 a carload, and the movie was *Valley of the Dolls*. There was a second feature called *The Spy with Me*.

Other than these little tidbits, there wasn't much else I could find about the Air Base Drive-in Theatre. My guess is it catered more to the military crowds than families.

ATLANTIC DRIVE-IN THEATRE

There were a number of drive-in theatres that I was able to attend as I was growing up. The Atlantic Drive-in was not the closest to my house, but it was not as far away as some that were across the river or at the beach. The Atlantic was, as I recall, one of the nicer drive-ins. I remember a very nice entryway that was lined with trees and required a sort of hairpin turn to get all the way inside. It had the obligatory playground down in the front. A Publix Super Market is on what was once the drive-in's property.

One of the most interesting stories about drive-ins was told to me by Jay Robinson, a retired investment broker who currently lives in San Marco. We met at the San Marco Starbucks and had a wonderful time reminiscing about our youth.

In 1947 or so, Robinson's father had just left the service in the navy, and he bought his family a home on Bartram Circle. Right behind their house was the Atlantic Drive-in Theatre. "In order to keep the peace," Robinson told me, "the owner of the drive-in dug a ditch and lay lines that were attached to speakers so that each house next to the drive-in could listen in on the movies if they wanted to. My dad and I built a flat-roofed garage, and he and I would use a ladder to get on top and watch about every movie that came to town."

Robinson remembered many movies, like *High Noon* with Gary Cooper and Grace Kelly, but the most memorable ones had titles he couldn't recall. They were Brigitte Bardot movies, and the titles were the last thing on his mind.

"When I was older and I began taking my girlfriends up on the garage to watch the movies, my mother, who was a great gal, would make hot chocolate and popcorn for us to take up there. Many wonderful memories!"

Another benefit Robinson found about being near the Atlantic Drive-in was income. "During the summer, my buddies and I would ride our bikes into the theatre during the day to find change that fell from people's pockets as they got in and out of their cars. We were searching for dimes, mostly. And we became friends with the caretaker who lived in an apartment in the screen. He got to take all the leftover popcorn home with him, and he'd share his stale popcorn with us. He even explained to us all about the facts of life, as I recall."

There were funny moments that the Robinson family witnessed. Every once in a while a car would roll up to the back of the property, and the driver would open the trunk only to have all these kids pour out.

CLEAR SAILING—Reflection of the sun causes a sparkling effect on lake in St. Louis during small sailboat race.

AP Wirephoto

Show Times

"COUNTERPOINT"—Charlton Heston. Five Points. Feature at 2, 4, 5:55, 7:55, 9:50.

"THE DEVIL'S BRIGADE" —William Holden. Center. Feature at 12, 2:25, 4:50, 7:15, 9:35.

"THE CARPETBAGGERS" —Carroll Baker. Florida. Feature at 1:20, 6:35. Also, "NEVADA SMITH" at 3:55, 9:10.

"YOURS, MINE AND OURS" — Lucille Ball. Regency. Feature at 1:45, 3:45, 5:50, 7:55, 10.

"STAY AWAY JOE"—Elvis Presley. Town and Country. Feature at 1:35, 3:40, 5:55, 7:50, 9:50.

Newspaper ad for the Atlantic Drive-in, *Jacksonville Journal*, June 5, 1968. *Personal collection.*

There were also the times when he and his friends would go through a gate in the back of the property, tiptoe up to some of the cars near the back—especially ones that were all fogged up—and pound on the windows to shake up the lovebirds.

I spoke with several other people who had fond memories of the Atlantic Drive-in. Jim Webb, who retired from the American Gold Exchange and lives in Arlington, would go to the movie with friends or his girl. Then, after "an evening at the movies, we turned onto Atlantic Boulevard and crossed over to Uncle Joe's Drive-in, or maybe we'd go in the opposite direction toward Love Grove Road and a soft-serve ice cream. Uncle Joe's was best known for its foot-long hot dogs for twenty-five cents, and a blue building where a plumbing business once operated stands in its place. Uncle Joe's had curb service in the back where the lights were dim, and that is where we often went to be alone with our girlfriends."

As with all good things, the Atlantic Drive-in passed on, and as the Publix shoppers make their rounds at the store on Atlantic Boulevard, they are probably unaware of what sacred ground they travel.

BEACHES DRIVE-IN THEATRE

I am not alone when I say I remember Beaches Drive-in Theatre, even though I am fairly certain I never went there as a patron. I definitely remember seeing it every time my family or I made the trek over the Intracoastal Waterway, down Beach Boulevard and to the sea. The drive-in was to our right on Shetter Avenue, and it had a badly faded Coca-Cola ad on it and the word "Drive-In" emblazoned at the top so there was no doubt what this building was.

I can just see it in my mind: a massive structure, a triangular building with no windows on the walls but with several doors around the bottom. One wall had been used as the screen, which I was told faced west, which made it difficult to start the movie until well after sundown. The whole thing was such a memorable building that when it was finally torn down, it was a noticeable loss.

In *Shorelines*, the beaches edition of the *Florida Times-Union*, on July 27, 2002, an article written by Caren Burmeister ran with the headline "Residents Want to keep Beaches Drive-In Screen." Todd Dunavant, who was an architect and a beach resident at the time, had done his master's

Beaches Drive-in Theatre not long before its demolition in 2003. *Courtesy of Betty McNamara.*

research project on the Beaches Drive-in. He spoke with a great deal of authority when he and others tried to convince the city and developers to preserve the fifty-two-foot screen.

At the time of the article, Art Kirshman was a partner with First Coast Commercial Realty, which had bought the property from the Cordray family. His company was planning to build a mini-warehouse facility on the grounds.

He said that he had been persuaded to protect the screen tower—for the moment, at least. He was quoted as saying, "There was a large outcry from the public. There's a lot of memories. People want to leave it there."

He also said that city planning officials had given him until the second phase of the warehouse development to decide what to do with the tower.

After the drive-in stopped functioning as such, it became the Seatlantic Mobile Home Park. The article said, "The homes were arranged along the fan shaped theater rows where customers had parked and hooked speakers to their car doors."

Sadly, Dunavant and others who wanted the screen's preservation were to be disappointed on July 7, 2003, when the *Beaches Leader* announced that the Beaches Drive-in screen tower was being torn down. In the article, it said the unstable portion had already been dislodged and the walls of the structure were to be "caved in as early as today."

Jacksonville Beach Planning and Development director Steve Lindorff was quoted as saying, "It's a non-conforming structure under our zoning code. It's too tall and too close to the property lines for a property zoned industrial. It was built before the code went into effect."

He went on to explain that the city had allowed Art Kirshman a "grace period," but all parties understood that for the old drive-in screen to stay, it had to be brought up to code or be brought down. Sadly, the old drive-in—built in 1950 by Fred Kent, made into a mobile home park in the '60s and a landmark for millions of beachgoers over the years—came tumbling down.

Memories of the place still exist. Tim Ballentine, a retired educator, said, "I do recall spending an evening on occasion at the Beaches Drive-in, but that was usually a family outing in my case. I do remember making numerous trips to the concession stand and being nosy—sneaking peeks in the projection room."

But mostly what people remember of the Beaches Drive-in Theatre is the huge building looming in the distance as if some sort of landmark. Such is the way of progress.

FOX DRIVE-IN THEATRE

When I was a young teacher and on my way to work at Edward H. White High School each day, I passed by the Fox Drive-in Theatre. Its marquee is about all I know personally of that drive-in, but when the organizers of the reunion of Ed White's class of 1975 contacted me about attending the reunion, I was able to ask some of my former students and teacher friends about what they recalled of the Fox.

Luisa Lawrence-Riseman, the president of the 1975 senior class of Edward H. White High School and presently living in Boston, told me in an e-mail:

> *The Fox Drive-in was the ultimate date night for Ed White students. I went there with my best friend from South Carolina and my boyfriend to watch* One Million Years B.C., *with Raquel Welch. I remember getting a laugh from them because when Raquel gets picked up by the pterodactyl and dropped into the ocean after a fight over her with another of his species, I said, "And her Timex Twistoflex watch is still ticking." Take that John Cameron Swayze!*
>
> *I also recall seeing* The Groove Tube *there, and that with one date (Mike Boone), he was smart enough to bring one of those mosquito coils so we didn't get "et up by skeeters." I also remember that when I went there with my date John, he walked me to the ladies' room (ah, romance). I was wearing my high-waisted jeans and a muslin striped green blouse and platform shoes. As I emerged from the ladies' room and walked toward him, he looked at me in a way where I thought he was totally taken aback by my beauty, but then he said, "Oh my gosh, you're bow-legged." Which I actually never knew until he pointed it out.*
>
> *On another occasion I went there with an eighteen-year-old date, Jimmy Lane from Orange Park High who recently moved to our neighborhood. The movie was no one under seventeen admitted. We knew I was going to say I was seventeen and that I had no ID. I have trouble lying (or I did then), and when we got to the ticket window, the guy asked my age and I said, "Sixteen." Jimmy looked at me like I was crazy, and we had to circle around the ticket booth and drive back out. He and his former girlfriend got back together not long after. She actually was over seventeen.*

Word spread that I was interested in Fox Drive-in stories, and I soon got an e-mail from Dale Cope, another '75 graduate. Cope said:

> *I have many fond memories of the Fox. Back in the day I used to go there pretty much every weekend. Sometimes in the backseat with the windows all fogged up with my date or other times sneaking in the trunk to avoid admission. Once some friends and I snuck in the back fence and simply sat down on the ground in the back and watched a movie. We got caught by*

security, and they asked us where our car was. We walked around awhile until he said, we didn't have any car, did we?

He called the cops on us, and when the cop came, it turned out to be my next-door neighbor. I asked him if he was going to take us to jail, and he said, "No, where do you guys want to go?" Then, he dropped us off in the neighborhood.

Elaine Mann, who is a retired educator, contacted me with her story. Even though she is not part of Ed White's class of '75 (I knew her through my connections to Wolfson Senior High School), I related to her story. She said:

Another girl and I were caught climbing out of the trunk at the Fox Drive-in. The reason we were in the trunk was we didn't have enough money for four. (Our dates rode up front.) We were taken to the office where the manager said we could pay, he could call our parents or he could call the police. We didn't have the money so that wasn't an option. Of the two remaining options, calling the police seemed the safest. "Call the police. Don't call my parents." In the end, he let us go and told us to bring the money back later. Days later we did, assuming we would have to give him the money and leave, but he let us watch the movie. On a side note, my mother had told me that if I lived to be one hundred, I was not allowed to go to a drive-in movie EVER! Only bad things happened there.

Charnisay Pickard Dauer, another Ed White Commander, had a great "sneak-in" story that I couldn't let pass. Dauer said:

The Fox Drive-in on Normandy is a place that brought me many fond memories. I always got a Hershey bar and popcorn (which I ate together; loved sweet and salty.) I had a '67 Dodge Charger and the backseats would fold down. Sneaked in a couple of people in the trunk, and they never had to get out to get into the main cabin (or pay admission). Remember the coiled stuff that smoked to keep out mosquitoes, and the static sound of the speaker that hung on the window? And makin' out with my favorite beau . . . those were the days!

Finally, Ruthanne Mason remembers when the Fox Drive-in was brand new and a first-run theatre. She said:

I saw Bambi *there when I was just the wrong age, when I didn't want anyone to see me cry. For years, my older brother would tease me and try to make me cry by saying, "Bambi! To the thicket!" And then, "We made it, Mother…Mother?" Yeah, it still gets me. Then, there was his story of going to all the trouble of sneaking someone in, in the trunk, and then finding out the price that night was by the carload. I remember a petition in the snack bar to try to keep cable television out of Jacksonville. I may have even signed it. Pay TV? Who wants that?*

After reading all of these stories, I am sorry that I only passed by the Fox Drive-in and never went there myself. It seems I missed an awful lot of fun.

MAIN STREET DRIVE-IN THEATRE

I don't suppose you could come up with a more American name than the Main Street Drive-in Theatre, nor could you find a better piece of Americana. Herman "Smitty" Shuman can certainly attest to the popularity of such a place because he worked there for many years—from 1956 to 1965. He started as the field-keeper and speaker-replacer. He then moved into the concession stand and became well known for his French fries and hot dogs on a stick. Next, he was the assistant manager until his boss, Bob Anderson, retired, and that is when he became a full manager.

"I absolutely loved working at the theatre. It was exciting, and I thoroughly enjoyed it," he said.

Shuman said that the theatre was owned by Fred Kent, who owned many other theatres around town, and that Kent was a very nice man. Shuman probably endeared himself to the man when he came up with a brilliant idea to get people into the theatre. It seemed that on Tuesdays, Wednesdays and Thursdays, hardly fifty cars would show up. The theatre wasn't breaking even. Since most of the theatre profits came from concessions, more patrons needed to come. So Shuman recommended that they let admission on those nights be ten cents a person, and Kent told him to go ahead and try it.

Tom Thompson, a motorcycle cop who used to come around and patrol the theatre area, called Shuman at home one afternoon around four o'clock and said that the cars were backed up down the street and around the block and that someone needed to get there fast. This new admission idea was a great success, and Kent rewarded Shuman with a four- or five-day vacation.

"My wife, my ten-year-old daughter, her friend and I got to go to Inverness, Florida, where Elvis Presley was filming *Follow That Dream*. We didn't get to

Aerial view of the Main Street Drive-in in the mid-twentieth century. *Courtesy of the Florida State Photographic Archives.*

see him during the day, but at night after dinner, Elvis would swim in the pool at our hotel. He was very nice to the little girls, who were thrilled."

Shuman had quite a few "bright ideas" during his time as manager at the Main Street Drive-in. During one Halloween, Shuman got Polly Ritter, a part-time employee, to pull a prank on patrons. First, he had a hearse on the property. Then he borrowed shipping box that resembled a coffin and put a cold turkey inside, leaving just enough of an opening to put a hand. Shuman asked if anyone was brave enough to touch a dead body. Polly volunteered and promptly pretended to faint. No one ever went near the coffin after that.

When the Lucy and Desi Arnaz movie called *The Long, Long Trailer* was playing, Shuman brought in a travel trailer and put it at the front of the property under the screen. Patrons could go inside and look around. When the Robert Mitchum movie *Thunder Road* was playing at the Main Street, Shuman got an authentic hot rod for people to see and touch.

Shuman also let local bands play in front of the concession stand or under the screen. He recalled a band called the Echoes and a local celebrity Toby Dowdy performing there. Dr. Wally Eaton said that the Classics played there. "I was seventeen and we often performed for free at this drive-in for a period of time before the movie feature got underway. These outdoor musical concerts were performed in the playground area of the theatre, just beneath the gigantic movie screen. We also would get cardboard pizzas and Pics products purchased at the refreshment stand. We'd light them up and hopefully their smoke would drive away mosquitoes."

For Eric Berman, who grew up in Jacksonville, the Main Street Drive-in is a vivid memory since he lived right across the street from it. In an e-mail, he told me about getting lost at the drive-in when he was very small and how he was in a panic until his father found him. He also told of a male babysitter who left him and his brothers alone only to find out that he had hopped the fence to the theatre to bring back concessions.

Finally, Berman said:

> *I remember going to Bob Buehl's house, which was actually on the theatre side of our street. We each had and were able to watch the Jacksonville-filmed movie* Creature from the Black Lagoon *while standing in Bob's backyard. As you know, one popular scene was the creature coming out of the river at the old Lobster House. We saw a couple of other movies at Bob's house, and I remember at least one movie with Indians being in 3-D, and we got a hold of the 3-D glasses, too; in fact, I believe the* Creature from the Black Lagoon *may have been one of them, but I couldn't swear to it. It was well over sixty years ago.*

Regardless of how long ago it was, places like the Main Street Drive-in still hold special places in our memories. For Herman Shuman, it was a wonderful place to be part of show business, and for others, like the garage bands of Jacksonville, it was a place to hone their craft. For Eric Berman it is a treasure-trove of memories, and for the rest of us, it was a great place to hang out and enjoy our little piece of heaven here in the good ole USA.

MIDWAY DRIVE-IN THEATRE

If the stories I have heard are true, the Midway Drive-in Theatre got its name by being "midway" between the city and Jacksonville Beach. It is probably close to the truth if you think about it, but now its space is a Walmart Supercenter, and all those glorious nights at the drive-in are just dim memories.

Patsy Groth Butterbrodt, a former Jacksonville resident who now lives in Tennessee, is someone who can remember this drive-in:

> *I remember Mom used to pop enough popcorn to fill a paper grocery bag, get four bottles of cold RC Cola, and the four of us (Mom; Dad; my brother, Andy; and I) would go to the drive-in on Beach Boulevard near Southside—I think there's a Walmart there now. We saw the early 007 movies, you know—the real James Bond, Sean Connery. We saw lots of Disney movies, like* Swiss Family Robinson *and* The Computer Wore Tennis Shoes, *starring a teenaged Kurt Russell. We also saw lots of westerns. At first my brother and I would fall asleep in the backseat when we were younger. As we grew—this was probably into the late '60s/early '70s—we made it through the whole movie.*

One of the most poignant things I discovered about the Midway Drive-in was a YouTube film, by a person identified as Valmrick60. The piece is a home movie entitled "Midway Drive In, Jacksonville, Fl 1986 super 8."

It may have been the music, or it may have been the familiar images now overgrown with weeds and full of potholes, but viewing the film left me with a bittersweet sensation as I watched—so many happy evenings for so many young people now just a busy hub of retail marketing. Progress is a good thing, but losing the Midway Drive-in still makes me feel a little sad.

NORMANDY TWIN DRIVE-IN THEATRE

Maggie Winstead O'Connor, a retired drama teacher and now a part-time actor, recalls that when she was a little girl living in Westside, she and her family went to the Normandy Twin Drive-in. "As I remember it, there was a little train that went all the way around the whole place, and they also had pony rides there—the kind that go in a circle. It was such a family place. Now it is where the Normandy Mall is."

Herb Fouraker wrote me in an e-mail about the Normandy Twin Drive-in saying,

> *My grandfather sold land to Herb Misselman for him to build the Normandy Twin Drive-in. Misselman's theatre group was called the Eastern Federal Theaters and included the St. Johns and either the Neptune or the Royal*

Aerial view of the Normandy Drive-in, 1948. *Courtesy of the Florida State Photographic Archives.*

> *Palms which were across the street from each other on Atlantic Boulevard at the Beach. The Normandy Twin was demolished to make way for the Normandy Mall, one of the early inside malls in Jacksonville.*

The *Breeze*, the Westside newspaper, reported in 1948 that the Normandy Twin Outdoor Theatre was a "70-foot structural steel, concrete block and asbestos tower." It was to be "completely fireproof and pitched at a 10 degree angle for improved visibility." It was also billed as "the largest in the South and the second largest in the nation."

It was going to have a 1,500-car capacity and an additional 1,000 seats for patrons in an enclosed seating facility. It was to open in the spring of 1949.

Patti Whiddon Walters, who grew up on the Westside, had a Normandy Twin story to share. "I remember my older sister and a bunch of her friends going to *The Exorcist*. My mom let me go with them. We even snuck people in, in the trunk! Then, we all sat all over the hood of the car with blankets and popcorn. So much fun, missed it when it closed!"

Michelle Raigosa, another person who grew up on the Westside, had a similar story. She said, "We would go see all the Disney movies! Go in pajamas, take Charles chip cans full of popcorn, Kool-Aid and candy. We would sit on the roof of our station wagon with pillows and blankets! A little boy was run over by his parents once, he was not hurt bad…we were really scared though! Spent many nights there as a teen, too. I think everyone put friends in the trunk at least once!"

According to a *Florida Times-Union* article written by Sue Dixon on June 19, 1991, the Normandy Shopping Mall was opened in 1969 after the drive-in closed, but in the mall was a theatre with two auditoriums called Normandy Twin Theatres.

By the late '90s, the mall was struggling and looking for a new buyer. Around 2007, the mall was purchased, and an article by Diana Middleton for the *Florida Times-Union* announced that Potter's House Christian Fellowship, a Westside mega church, had purchased the mall. It boasted a bowling alley, eatery and gym, and it had space that could be rented out for events. Middleton said that any money left after expenses would go to mission work.

Kingdom Mall, as the Normandy Mall is now called, still operates today, and the drive-in is now in the distant past.

SOUTHSIDE DRIVE-IN THEATRE

Back in the late '40s, during a time when the corner of Philips Highway and University was in the "boonies," an Amoco Filling Station stood sentinel, waiting to serve customers who might venture out that far. The property was owned by Joseph Ripley, and sadly, the gas station just couldn't attract enough customers to be a viable concern. Lucky for us in Jacksonville, the closing of the filling station set the stage for one of the most beloved drive-in theatres in the area—the Southside Drive-in Theatre.

Ripley owned a considerable portion of the property on that corner, and sometime around 1952 or '53, Ripley built a drive-in theatre for Fred Kent, the owner of some sixty theatres in Florida. Ripley leased the Southside Drive-in Theatre to Kent until the theatre closed and was demolished in 1980.

Joe Ripley, the son of Joseph and a lawyer who has been practicing in Jacksonville for over fifty years, loved this drive-in. "I think I went to every movie that ever played there since I had free passes. And my father provided the place with a wonderful playground for the kids. Those were some good days."

When Joseph died in 1968, his son, Joe, inherited the property and continued to lease these properties to the concerns mentioned.

Darian McIntyre Hulslander, a Jacksonville resident, told me, "The Southside Drive-in was ten minutes from my home so we went to that one the most. Mostly on dates. Loved intermission when we would get out and go car to car to talk with friends. We'd go to Burger King, buy burgers and fries and take them with us! Also, we'd fall asleep sometimes and have the manager come tap on our window to leave!"

Nancy Lockwood Forbes, who grew up on the Southside, had one of the best stories. She told me:

> *I remember being in my mother's Lincoln and sitting in front near Pat Garner's house and smoking a cigarette. Guess who drives by but my mother! My mother waved at us and had this little smile on her face. Halfway through the first movie an announcement came through the speaker. I had an emergency at home and needed to call right away. It was my mother! She told me to come right home. I dropped off my friends and went home. She took away the car for a month! Things at the drive-in just got more interesting after that. Including corrupting my brother by taking him and his girlfriend to the drive-in and paying their way on my five-dollar allowance. I would leave them and sneak out with friends! Movie over and would sneak back in to get them. Some of the best moments of growing up!*

Betsy Bier, a former resident of Arlington mentioned earlier, met her husband at the Southside when she was a junior at Terry Parker:

> *I remember that I was at a slumber party, and we all decided that we wanted to go to the movies. Some of us wanted to go to a walk-in movie and the rest of us wanted to go to the drive-in. Funny, I can't remember what the film was—maybe it was something like* Billy Jack*. I don't remember. But I'll never forget that car of guys we walked past on the way to the concession stand. They had a oogha horn and some kind of PA system where we could hear their comments, and we thought they were so cute.*
>
> *We made up some story about how we were college girls, but we were busted when one of the guys had a Wolfson club jersey that one of the girls recognized. So after that we all sat around and talked, and Doug and I just really hit it off.*

On a bright, sunny day in 1980, the Southside Drive-in was demolished. The *Florida Times-Union* was there to capture the passing of a Southside

The demolition of the Southside Drive-in, 1980. *Courtesy of the* Florida Times-Union.

favorite, and many of us can't help but turn our heads every time we pass the place as we travel down University Boulevard or up Philips Highway. I suppose it is a matter of respect or maybe it's the hope that the skyline will have changed. But no, that's just wishful thinking.

WESTCONNETT/TWIN HILLS/PLAYTIME DRIVE-IN THEATRES

I often wonder about the quality of a place. Some places are so serene, and others are filled with many difficulties. And I wonder about the place where the Westconnett Drive-in, the Twin Hills Drive-in and the Playtime Drive-in were. Located in the fork of Blanding and Westconnett Boulevards, this area became the location for some very interesting activities.

On June 24, 1955, an article ran in the *Breeze* in which it was announced that the Westconnett Drive-in on Blanding Boulevard was about 75 percent complete. Then, a week later on July 1, the newspaper showed a dramatic picture of a damaged drive-in screen and scaffolding strewn all around. It was all the result of "last Sunday's 70–80 mile winds" that had passed through the Westside neighborhood.

Thankfully, the summer of 1955 passed without further incident for the new theatre. The *Breeze* announced on September 26, 1955, that the screen had been completed, the speakers had been installed, the equipment for the concession stand was to be installed that very week and, in the very near future, the new Westconnett Drive-in would be opened for business.

After some calculations, since I couldn't find an article about the actual opening, I figured that September 30 and October 1 were the days of the opening weekend of the new theatre, since the first movie to play there was *Ten Wanted Men*, starring Randolph Scott. It was to show on a Friday and Saturday night, and the dates would be appropriate to that year.

The drive-in also had a second feature, and the source I had did not have the name of the movie. It only had the blurb for the movie, which said, "a redhead from nowhere and a stop-at-nothing guy." Already, anyone can tell that this place was going to be interesting.

Eventually, the Westconnett Drive-in showed some interesting films that should have foretold its later incarnation. In the '50s when these movies were shown, my guess would be that most families would decline an evening at a place showing movies like these: *Naughty New Orleans*, with a tag line that said, "Women out to get every thrill," and *Swamp Women*, with the tag line saying "Scarlet Women with a Lust for Men."

In the year 1960, the Westconnett Drive-in became the Twin Hills Drive-in. On June 2, 1960, a headline in the *Breeze* announced "Twin Hills Drive-in Makes Bow after Old Theatre Is Remodeled." The new owner of the property, according to the article, was Cecil P. Cohen, who also owned Murray Hill Theatre on Edgewood Avenue. This drive-in was to "bring the finest in current feature attractions for theatre-goers of our community." On opening night, the movie was *Sink the Bismarck*, starring Kenneth More and Dana Wynter.

As often happens when one does research, I discovered discrepancies between my sources. According to an article written for the *Florida Times-Union* by Adam Aasen and published on May 31, 2008, the Playtime Drive-in started its life as the Twin Hills Drive-in in 1948. Both the date and the original name are different from what was reported by the *Breeze*.

Aasen's account of the third name change in the early '70s—to the Playtime Drive-in Theatre showing X-rated films—seems plausible since the *Breeze* had stopped publishing in the mid-'70s and, therefore, wasn't around to report on its change in format. One thing Aasen's account provides is a rare look into a world about which most of us Jacksonville teenagers only snickered and made jokes. The article said:

> *A* [Jacksonville] *city ordinance banned nudity at drive-in theatres, which was overturned by the U.S. Supreme Court in a 5–4 decision in 1975.*
>
> [Manager Marty] *Hamrick, 48, began running the projector 22 years ago during the X-rated days. He remembers cross-dressers and police raids and having to put his hand over the projector during the hardcore scenes banned by the ordinance.*
>
> *Playtime eventually switched back to just showing family fare in the early 80s.*

It was in May 2008 that the Playtime Drive-in showed its last movie, the newest Indiana Jones film (probably *Indiana Jones and the Kingdom of the Crystal Skull*). But that last show was not the end of the Playtime Drive-in's story.

The ownership of the drive-in and attached flea market had gone to Christ Church Anglican. Then, in what many of us would consider an ironic kind of twist, the church found a cache of porn films in one of the upper rooms of the concession stand. In a symbolic gesture, the church planned to burn the films and cleanse the area in a rather public way. Apparently, that brought them to the attention of NPR, National Public Radio.

If you go to NPR's website (http://www.npr.org/templates/story/story.php?storyId=95913049), you can hear the actual broadcast of the interview with senior pastor Mark Eldredge of Christ Church Anglican. It seemed to me that the dilemma that existed for the church had many layers.

First, the church had no use for these films. Then, they didn't think it right to profit from these movies by selling them, and finally, they didn't want them circulating in the community. So they burned them at a kind of festival/picnic event, and the fire department was there so that no one would get hurt. In any case, if these films were all that rare, someone would have taken them when the format changed. Besides, the drive-in had gone back to its family-friendly status in the '80s, some thirty years earlier.

I spoke on the phone with Patricia Rioux, the administrative assistant of Christ Church Anglican, to get an insider's take on the most recent iteration of this drive-in area. Of the church's purchase of a drive-in theatre, she said, "It was about reclaiming the land, and we thought we might actually build a church here. And we had such great visions. It was an awesome time when everyone was excited and it was a real celebration."

Even now, the church owns the property and the adjoining flea market area (and Rioux says they are motivated sellers, if anyone were to be interested in buying). They still use the space for Wednesday night Bible study, and they have bazaars there occasionally. But for the most part, the buildings are dilapidated.

"We got a lot of negative feedback concerning our 'film burning' activity, but in actuality, the films were in awful shape. They had been left in these crumbling buildings, they were sticky—unusable, so the burning was symbolic. We had hoped to show a new direction for a sad place."

Rioux went on to tell of an e-mail that Father Eldridge received from a woman who had been involved in the pornography trade. She was very grateful that the church was disposing of those films and the memory of that horrible life in which she had been involved.

Rioux also said, "We had planned to operate a drive-in as a source of revenue—we would show current films, and we would make money through concessions. We weren't even going to charge anything to get in; but nobody came. We were amazed by that, and after we spent considerable money to show three or so movies, we had to abandon our dream."

The church has since found a new and better facility at 9917 103rd Street, and that is now the church's permanent home. Hopefully, the church can sell the drive-in/flea market property and move its dreams in a different direction. Still, I marvel at how a revered and an infamous place can be such a source of fascination in Jacksonville's theatre history.

CONCLUSION

Now comes the part when the words "The End" are splashed across the screen. The credits begin to roll and the lights slowly come up or the headlights click on. People then begin their slow walk or drive back to their lives and a world without tidy endings and well-planned plots. The drive-ins may be no more. The movie theatres now are usually of the multiplex variety, and concerts and plays still unfold "dramatically" all over the northeast Florida area.

I take comfort, as I hope you do, that the movie/play/concert experience is still very much part of the Jacksonville landscape. Many revered theatres can rest easy in our hearts, and we can rest assured that the show will always go on. We are lucky to have so many memorable theatres, and it seems that even now people are making new memories in the theatres that still remain.

Ticket stubs from Jacksonville theatres. *Personal collection.*

BIBLIOGRAPHY

Aasen, Adam. "Drive-In's Last Show." *Florida Times-Union*, May 31, 2008.

Barry, John R. "Public Dedicates Civic Auditorium." *Florida Times-Union*, September 17, 1962.

Bauerlein, David. "$225,000 Restoration Project Will Restore Façade of Historic Florida Theatre." *Florida Times-Union*, April 9 2015.

Beach News and Advertiser. News brief about a barbershop fire. August 26, 1964.

Breeze. News brief about Normandy Twin Drive-in Theatre. 1948.

———. News brief about the completion of Westconnett Drive-in. September 26, 1955.

———. News brief about the Westconnett Drive-in. June 24, 1955.

———. "Twin Hills Drive-in Makes Bow after Old Theatre Is Remodeled." June 2, 1960.

Bull, Roger. "Alhambra Dinner Theatre Closes: May Not Be Final Act." *Florida Times-Union*, August 31, 2009.

Burmeister, Caren. "Residents Want to Keep Beaches Drive-in Screen: Shetter Avenue Tower a Symbol of Old Times." *Florida Times-Union*, July 27, 2002.

Bussard, Dick. "City's 'Theatre Row' Is No More." *Jacksonville Journal*, September 27, 1971.

———. "5 Points Theatre: The Innovator." *Jacksonville Journal*, January 13, 1977.

———. "When the Nickelodeon Was in Flower." *Jacksonville Journal*, May 15, 1975.

Cornelius, Elizabeth. "Love of Painting Comes in Handy for Florida Theatre Renovation." *Florida Times-Union*, October, 3, 1983.

Craig, James C. "Old Circular Stirs Memories of Park Opera House's Glory." *Florida Times-Union*, November 28, 1948.

Crumpler, David. "Curtain Up! River City Playhouse Comes to Five Points." *Florida Times-Union*, November 5, 1984.

———. "Curtain Up: Theatre Group Crosses River to New Location." *Florida Times-Union*, May 21, 1984.

———. "Theater Reopening." *Jacksonville Journal*, August 14, 1981.

Dixon, Drew. "Theater Ends Run as Church Takes Its Place." *Shorelines Edition, Florida Times-Union*, April 4, 2007.

Dixon, Sue. "Mall Looking for Big Spender—To Buy It." *Florida Times-Union*, June 19, 1991.

Elmore, Frank H. "Judge Ushered at Palace Opening." *Jacksonville Journal*, November 4, 1971.

Florida Times-Union. "Closing Set Tomorrow by St. Johns Theatre." September 17, 1960.

———. "Coliseum Dedication Set Today: Exhibitions of Sports Events to Follow Ceremonies." November 24, 1960.

———. "Coliseum Rising." June 5, 1959.

———. "Construction Is Started on New Murray Hill Theatre." December 12, 1948.

———. "Five Points' New Theatre Open Tonight." August, 11, 1949.

———. "Hearing Music as We've Never Heard It Before." September 16, 1962.

———. "Kirk Veto Is Asked on Liquor License." June 28, 1967.

———. "Landmark Theatre Closes Its Doors." January 13, 1977.

———. "New Drive in Theatre Opens." September 4, 1948.

———. "Officers of New Plaza Theatre." January 15, 1967.

———. "Regency Square Movie Theatre to Bow Jan. 18." December 24, 1967.

———. "Theatre Runs Own Nursery for 23 Years." September 10, 1950.

———. "You're Invited." September 16, 1962.

Foley, Bill. "Edgewood Theatre Kept 1950s Alive Awhile." *Florida Times-Union*, April 24, 1988.

———. "Razing of Old Dixie Theatre Begins." *Florida Times-Union*, September 3, 1964.

———. "St. Johns Theatre Illuminated Downtown." *Florida Times-Union*, September 17, 1960.

Gardner, Shirley Jordan. "Memories of Another Movie Theatre Years Ago." *Metropolis*, February 9, 1983.

Gould, Sharon. "Then and Now." *Times/Journal* Sunday Magazine, September 25, 1966.

———. "Then and Now." *Times/Journal* Sunday Magazine, January 15, 1967.

Halton, Beau. "The Last Picture Show." *Jacksonville Journal*, January 6, 1983.

Hyman, Ann. "Remembering the Man at the Wurlitzer." *Florida Times-Union*, March 5, 1992.

Jacksonville Journal. "Do You Remember When You Went to the Movies in This Theatre?" December 31, 1937.

Kerr, Jessie-Lynne. "Don Curtis, Pro Wrestling's 'Buffalo Bomber' Became a Promoter: The Pro Wrestler Spent Many of His Later Years Working for the City." *Florida Times-Union*, March 8, 2008.

Khairullah, Natasha. "Five Points Theatre Packs Park Street." *Financial News and Daily Record*, June 26, 2007.

Lewis, Carol L. "Group Seeks to Put Glitz Back on Ritz." *Florida Times-Union*, November 9, 1986.

———. "La Villa: Much of Jacksonville's Black History Is Being Lost to the Bulldozer." *Florida Times-Union*, November 9, 1986.

Marden, William E. "Old Theatre Assumes New Role." *Jacksonville Journal*, October 1, 1984.

May, Judge. "Debut Set Tonight by Center Theatre." *Florida Times-Union*, August 3, 1960.

———. "Five Points Making Ready for Cinerama." *Florida Times-Union,* October 29, 1961.

———. "San Marco Is Successful in Switching to Art Films." *Florida Times-Union*, October 25, 1962.

———. "Spectacular 'Ben-Hur' Opens Center Theatre." *Florida Times-Union*, August 7, 1960.

McGee, Tom. *The Girl with the Million Dollar Legs*. Vestal, NY: Vestal Press, Ltd., 1995.

Middleton, Diana. "The Mall God Built." *Florida Times-Union*, September 2, 2007.

Mitchell, Tia. "Partial Collapse Speeds Demise of Center Theatre." *Florida Times-Union*, September 6, 2002.

Moewe, M.C. "Locals Plan to Restore Former Five Points Theatre." *Florida Times-Union*, September 1, 2004.

NPR Broadcast. "Florida Church Burns X-Rated Film Reels." October 20, 2008. http://www.npr.org/templates/story/story.php?storyId=95913049.

Ocean Beach Reporter. "'Beach Theatre' to Open This Week." July 17, 1936.

Parker, Yvonne. "Ticket Sales Warm Chilly Opera House." *Florida Times-Union*, December 27, 1964.

Patterson, Steve. "Makeover in the Works for Summer." *Florida Times-Union*, February 10, 1996.

Patton, Charlie. "Ritz Opens to Raves." *Florida Times-Union*, September 22, 1999.

Phelps, Bob. "Homecoming for Historic Music Mansion." *Florida Times-Union*, March 29, 1998.

Rhoades, Shirrel. "First Casting for a First Theatre." *Times/Journal* Sunday Magazine, December 10, 1967.

———. "Opening at the Alhambra Is a Posh Theatrical Banquet." *Florida Times-Union*, December 15, 1967.

Rogers, Jonathan. "Opening Night Rousing Success." *Florida Times-Union*, October 2, 1983.

Saisselin, Numa. "A Symbol of Hope: A History of the Florida Theatre." 2014.

Soergel, Matt. "The 5 Points Theatre Takes Offbeat Path." *Florida Times-Union*, November 15, 2009.

———. "Renovated 5 Points Theatre to Open This Week as Sun-Ray Cinema." *Florida Times-Union*, December 5, 2011.

———. "San Marco Theatre Turns 75." *Florida Times-Union*, June 7, 2013.

"A Town All Worked Up." *Life*, 1956: 108–9.

The 2013–2014 Yearbook of the Friday Musicale of Jacksonville, Florida. Jacksonville, FL, 2013, 18.

Wisckol, Martin. "Ritz Theatre Dream Becoming a Reality." *Florida Times-Union*,

December 22, 1994.
Woodhouse, Johnny. "Bit of the Past Going: Landmark Drive-in Screen from the '50s Being Torn Down." *Beaches Leader*, July 9, 2003.
———. "Brown Screened Early Version of 'Endless Summer' at the Beach Theatre in 1964." *Beaches Leader*, May 2006.
Valmrick60. "Midway Drive In, Jacksonville, Fl1986 Super 8." YouTube.com.

INDEX

R

S

T

U

V

W

Z

ABOUT THE AUTHOR

Dorothy K. Fletcher retired from the Duval County Public School System in 2007 after thirty-five years of teaching English classes. She was then able to embrace her passion—writing. Her monthly column, "By the Wayside," which she wrote for the *Florida Times-Union*, led to a series of history books she has written about her beloved home, Jacksonville, Florida. She and her husband, Hardy, love traveling and hanging out with their grandchildren.